South African American Confederate Pensioners 1923–1925

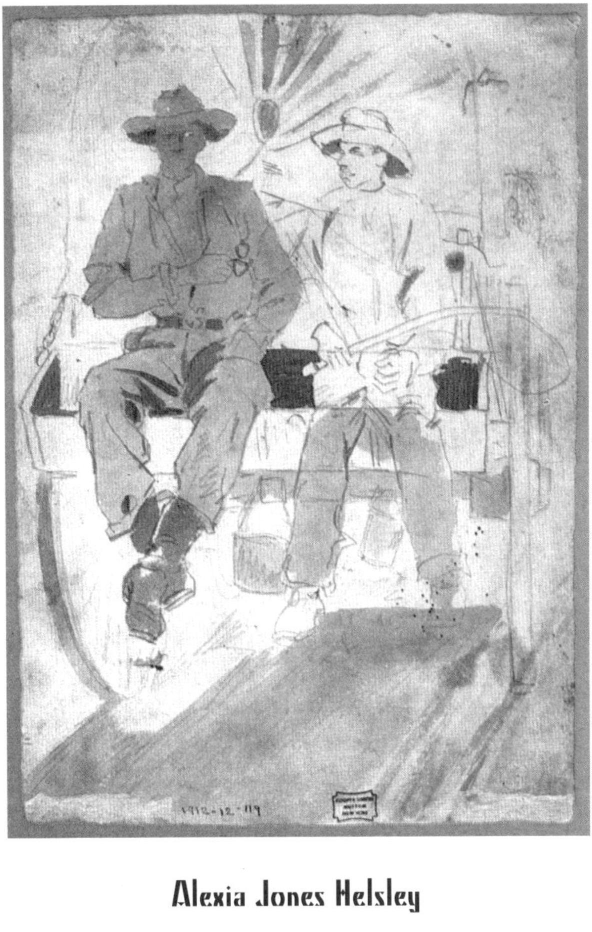

Alexia Jones Helsley

South Carolina Department of Archives and History

Editor and designer: Judith M. Andrews

Acknowledgements

Many thanks to Lee Drago of our Publications Advisory Board, who suggested this publication. The author gratefully acknowledges the assistance of Dolly Wells, Ruth Green, Marion Chandler, Garry Davis, Judith Andrews, and Tim Belshaw. Also, Patrick McCawley shared his Civil War records expertise, and Joseph Gainey contributed material on upstate pensioners.

Title page: "Two Men in Army Wagon," 1862. Winslow Homer, American, 1836–1910. Graphite and gray wash on cream wove paper. 239 x 169 mm (9 7/16 x 6 5/8 inches). Cooper-Hewitt, National Design Museum, Smithsonian Institution/Art Resource, NY. Gift of Charles Savage Homer, 1912-12-1919.

Contents

Dedicated
to
Uel Henry Jones
who also values South Carolina's
rich and diverse history

Introduction

History's heroes are many, but often little remembered. This publication details the Civil War service of a group of African Americans. In 1860 South Carolina's population included 291,300 white, 402,206 slave, and 9,914 free African Americans. The majority of the South Carolina work force was African American.

Background

Signing the Ordinance of Secession and firing the shot on Fort Sumter drove South Carolina to war. By 1862, visions of a short conflict, of peaceful coexistence with the Union, and of formal European intervention on behalf of the Confederate States had dimmed. South Carolina and the other Confederate States faced a lengthy struggle for survival.

South Carolina needed labor—to support combat troops, to construct and maintain fortifications, to man essential industries, and to produce the foodstuffs to supply military and domestic needs. Since 1720, South Carolina's agricultural economy had been dependent upon African American labor. By 1860, African Americans still constituted the backbone of South Carolina's agriculture but also worked as brick masons, carpenters, in other trades, and as pilots, stevedores, and boat hands.

Within this context of dependence, South Carolina organized for war. With secession and the South Carolina Constitution of 1860, South Carolina viewed herself as an independent nation. On 30 December 1860, Gov. Francis W. Pickens constituted the first Executive Council. This council included a secretary of state, a postmaster general, a secretary of war, a secretary of the treasury, and a secretary of the interior.[1] This first (1861) Executive Council functioned as an advisor to Gov. Pickens. It held its last recorded meeting on 23 March.

On 7 January 1862, the Secession Convention passed an ordinance to establish the second Executive Council. To meet changing conditions within the state, it "virtually supplanted [Gov. Pickens] as the state executive authority."[2] Federal troops had captured Port Royal harbor, and Beaufort and other coastal areas lay behind enemy lines. A disastrous fire had broken out in Charleston, and South Carolina's leaders daily expected a Federal attack upon that city. This 1862 council vigorously mobilized for war until the South Carolina legislature abolished it on 18 December 1862.[3] Of major concern was manpower for the coastal defenses. The Council's minutes bear eloquent testimony to the dangers it perceived and to its efforts to meet the challenges.

By March 1862, Gen. R. S. Ripley was impressing low-country African Americans to complete fortifications around Charleston. Slaves between the ages of sixteen and fifty were eligible for impressment, but only one-fourth of an individual's work force could be taken at one time. Similarly, Col. A. M. Manigault was impressing slaves in the Georgetown area to obstruct the mouth of Winyah Bay. Maj. Gen. John C. Pemberton, general in command at Pocotaligo, was requisitioning slaves to complete fortifications there.[4]

The scope of the task and fear of imminent Federal advance created a steadily increasing demand for labor. On 27 April 1862, Ripley wrote Gov. Pickens:

> If you want me to go on with the works in the harbor as the necessity of the time requires, you must send labor as fast as you can. I want a thousand negroes.[5]

Without centralized coordination, the haphazard impressment produced inequities. Some owners procrastinated or avoided compliance; others saw their workers impressed and retained beyond their terms of service. On 5 May, Gov. F. W. Pickens proclaimed martial law over the City of Charleston within a ten-mile radius and authorized the "Confederate General commanding in South Carolina" to impress labor for "public works and defence" in the Parishes of St. James Santee, St. Stephen's, St. John's Berkeley, St. Thomas and St. Denis, Christ Church, St. Andrew's, St. George Dorchester, St. James Goose Creek, St. Bartholomew, Prince William's, St. Luke's, and St. Peter. On 26 June, the Executive Council asked Gov. Pickens to issue a proclamation asking owners who had not contributed to send a fourth of the slaves "liable to road duty." In August, the Council extended the call for African American labor from the countryside to include incorporated municipalities.[6]

The Council and Gen. Pemberton, Confederate general commanding in South Carolina, disagreed about the scope of labor impressment. Pemberton wanted it statewide, while the Council preferred to limit it to the affected areas. By July, Pemberton had prevailed.[7] At least 1800 men were requisitioned at a time,[8] and service was usually for a month. A Newberry resident complained in October, however, that impressed African Americans were being held on the coast beyond their terms.

On 18 December 1862, the South Carolina legislature passed Act #4614, creating a state agent to oversee African American labor raised under the act.[9]

In general, Confederate forces employed African Americans in limited capacities. Many served as cooks or servants, but, as already discussed, the state also drew large numbers to build coastal fortifications and man essential industries. A letter accompanying the petition of Ben P. Griffin of Pickens mentions that Griffin was sent by his master "by the request of Gov. Pickens for labor" to Fort Sumter. Confederates used impressed labor to free white men for military service. In military camps, African Americans served as teamsters, cooks, and general servants. Towards the end of the Civil War, the Confederate Congress considered using African Americans as auxiliary forces, but South Carolina never adopted that proposal.

The Pension Records[10]

The South Carolina Confederate pension applications abstracted here were tendered under the act of 1923. Although South Carolina provided a short-lived disability compensation in 1866 and pension relief for regular Confederate soldiers as early as 1887, the state did not recognize the service of South Carolina's African Americans until 1923. At least four African Americans, M. F. Wharton (Abbeville County), Benjamin Chisolm (Berkeley County), July Galluchat (Clarendon County), and Andrew Richardson (Richland County), applied under the act of 1887.[11]

On 16 March 1923, the legislature approved "An Act to Provide for Pensions for certain faithful Negroes who were engaged in the service of the State in the War between the States." Under the act (Act 63), African Americans who served the Confederacy as "servants, cooks or attendants" were eligible for a pension. Additional qualifications included at least six months of service and the recommendation of the County Pension Board. These pensions could not exceed $25 annually.

Many African Americans applied under the 1923 act. In 1924, however, the act was amended to include only South Carolina residents who served the state at least six months as servants or cooks. This provision eliminated laborers, teamsters, and those who served from other states, and laborers impressed for work on the fortifications. Made ineligible by this act were men like Jake Gantt of Aiken, who served as a laborer for the Fourth Tennessee Regiment, and Alfred Grant of Laurens, whose petition was granted in 1923 and subsequently revoked.[12]

The 1923 petitions often give the type and location of service in detail. Louis Pou of Orangeburg "hauled supplies from the Livingston Mill at Beaver Creek for shipment to troops at Charleston." William Hook, also from Orangeburg, constructed breastworks on James Island, on Sullivan's Island, and at "Hampton's race track near Columbia." Henry Williams of Greenville "served with Major William Hay at Charleston, South Carolina making salt for distribution among the people of upper South Carolina."

Many of the laborers served in different parts of the state, but the activities of the servants often involved considerably more mobility. Benjamin Singleton of Beaufort began his service as a servant to Captain John H. Thompson and continued with him until Thompson was killed at the Battle of Second Manassas. Singleton then served under Sergeant William Thompson and Corporal David Thompson in the Beaufort Volunteers "until after the battle of Honey Hill." Singleton ended the war serving under Robert and James Thompson with the Citadel Cadets and "Columbia School Boys."

Other petitioners engaged in specialized service. W. S. Lewis, from Charleston, was James Thurston's servant in the Marine Corps aboard the CSS *Atalanta,* and William Sanders of Barnwell served Dr. J. B. Baxley, "a surgeon in the army in charge of the Third Georgia Hospital, Augusta, Georgia." Several of the petitions mention wounds suffered by the petitioners while in Confederate service. J. K. Knight from Oconee was wounded at Petersburg in 1864. Spencer Copeland of Laurens injured a foot while digging barefoot on the breastworks at Charleston. His leg was later amputated. July Galluchat of Clarendon, one of the 1887 petitioners whose petition survives, had both his left leg and left hand amputated.

The petitions of personal servants often contain poignant references to the circumstances of their service. Anthony Watts from Laurens served until his master died from battle wounds, and then Watts transported the body home. Zack Brown of Fairfield was servant to Robert F. Coleman until Coleman was injured—then Brown "stayed with him in hospital 'til it was captured." Wade Childs of Anderson served Captain Cothran in Orr's Rifles. When Cothran was wounded at Second Manassas, Childs courageously carried him on his back to the rear of the battle line.

Three petitioners professed to have served in a military regiment: Tom Bing of Hampton as a "private soulder" in Colcock's Regiment under Captain Bill Peeples; Tom Arch of Spartanburg as a private in Co. B, 1st SC Cavalry; John McKinley, private in Charleston riflemen, 14th Regiment. Unfortunately, no substantiating data has been found. One woman, Lavinia Thompson of Aiken, drew a pension for her service as a cook. Another woman, Nina L. Brown of Sumter, received a widow's pension (Appendix A). One of the more involved applications belongs to Jacob Washington of Hampton. His application contains considerable information about his life. Washington was born in 1844 and by age twelve was a house servant. In 1861 he accompanied Peter Craddock as cook and hostler in camp at Pocataligo. "When the yankee taken Bay Point and Beaufort," however, Washington took his "mistress" to refuge. Later Craddock joined Hampton's Legion, and Washington followed him until Lee's surrender. Washington succinctly described the aftermath of the war: "after surrender we came Home and made a crop on the Place after which we parted and He went to St. Augustine."

These applications and supporting documentation contain useful information. Some petitions show evidence of name changes—William Hook was known as William Dannelly during the Civil War, and James Burton of Beaufort served as Larkin Burton. Some petitions have information about former owners and other family connections: James Stoutamire certified that he married the mistress of Joseph Bunch, petitioner from Orangeburg. The applications also bear occasional evidence of the health and literacy of the petitioner.

About this publication

The pension applications abstracted here were submitted by the County Pension Boards to the South Carolina Comptroller General[13] between 1919 and 1925. Not all counties are covered. The applications are filed by county and indexed on Computer Output Microfilm (COM). In preparing this publication, staff examined each application individually and located information on several individuals who were not included on the COM index. The names of those excluded from the COM index are marked with an asterisk (*) in the text.

The abstracts

The applications for pensions under the acts of 1923 and 1924 required the following information: the petitioner's name, his address, the outfit with which he served, the captain or other officer under whom he served, his length of service, and the signatures of character references. The abstracts contain relevant information from those applications. Also included, if found, is an abstract of the pensioner's death certificate. The abstracts are arranged in alphabetical order, and the information is included as submitted; no attempt was made to verify unit designations or officer names. Names of the pensioners, because they are in alphabetical order, are not indexed. Names appearing within the abstracts are indexed.

The appendices

This publication also includes four appendices.

The first is on Nina L. Brown, widow.

The second, in alphabetical order by county, is the comptroller general's pension list for 1926—the first to list African American recipients by name. Names in this appendix are listed alphabetically under each county. Names in this appendix not included in the abstracts have been indexed. The other names have not.

The third is on Frank Rangs.

The fourth, in alphabetical order by pensioner, reproduces census SOUNDEX information on applicants. Applicants' names in this appendix are not indexed, but names within the entries are.

Additional information

Additional information and later applications for pensioners not listed here may be found with the records of the County Pension Boards. The Archives holds county pension records for Anderson, Clarendon, Charleston, Fairfield, Horry, Kershaw, Lexington, Pickens, Spartanburg, Union, and York. Other county records should be found in the county of origin.

Possible sources of additional information on the pensioners listed here include the Federal census schedules, 1870–1920; the 1869 Militia Enrollments; the 1868 Voter Registrations; death certificates, and available county records. For more detailed suggestions, please see *African American Genealogical Research* by Paul R. Begley, Alexia J. Helsley and Steven D. Tuttle (South Carolina Department of Archives and History, 1997) and *Guide to Civil War Records* by Patrick McCawley (South Carolina Department of Archives and History, 1994).

These applicants do not appear in the South Carolina Rolls of Provisional Troops nor in the Compiled Service Records of Confederate Soldiers from South Carolina. Consequently, these applications constitute one of the few sources on the Confederate service of South Carolina's African Americans. The records of these men and women offer unique insights into the complexities of racial interdependence in Civil War South Carolina.

Notes

1. *Journals of the South Carolina Executive Councils of 1861 and 1862,* ed. Charles E. Cauthen. The State Records of South Carolina (Columbia: South Carolina Archives Department, 1956), x.
2. Ibid.
3. Ibid., xii.
4. Ibid., 105, 111, 114–15.
5. Ibid., 160
6. Ibid., 166, 248–49, 278, 308, 2165.
7. Ibid., 183, 216, 221, 233, 240, 281.
9. Another source that documents the Civil War service of South Carolina's African Americans are the Records of the State Auditor. The State Auditor's annual reports list claims allowed for slaves who died in public service. These claims often include the name of the deceased, the name of the owner, the dates of impressment and occasionally, the date and cause of death. In November 1863 James Tupper, State Auditor, reported approved claims totalling $218,100 for "slaves lost in the public service." Report of the State Auditor, *Reports and Resolutions.*
10. The following discussion is based, in part, upon "Black Confederates" by Alexia J. Helsley which appeared under Notes and News from the Archives in the *South*

Carolina Historical Magazine, LXXIV (1973), 184–87.
11. Report of the Pension Board, *Reports and Resolutions,* 1888, vol. 1, 506.
12. R. Burton Hicks, probate judge for Spartanburg County, wrote to the comptroller general's office on 17 June 1924, asking him to strike the following names from the Spartanburg County pension roll "as they went in as laborers or were not cooks nor servants": Simpson Alexander, Simp Foster, Albert Gray, Darty Winn, Prince Reeder, and Dave Cunningham. Confederate Pension Applications, 1919–1926, #1111b, Records of SC Comptroller General.
13. The annual reports of the comptroller general, who supervised the pension system, give the total appropriations and expenditures for African American and white pensioners. In 1924, for example, the state appropriated $750,000 for white pensions and expended $744,672.85. For the same period, $3,000 was designated for African American pensions and $2,840 spent. In 1946, the last appropriation for African American pension relief was made, but none of the $75 allotted was expended. Annual Report of the Comptroller General for 1924, *Reports and Resolutions,* 1925; Annual Report of the Comptroller General for 1946, *Reports and Resolutions,* 1947.

A

ABEL, Anderson
Columbia, Richland County
Cook under Ed Mobley, Co. G, 6th Regt Cav
Served June 186? – October 1864
Applied 15 May 1924; approved 15 May 1924
Affidavit: J. W. McCreight and L. W. Taylor
Application #9850: Anderson Able, widower, 80 years old, died 15 January 1927 in Fairfield County. Able was a farmer and the son of S. and Julia Able. Informant—Charlie Alston, Ridgeway, SC *(SC Bureau of Vital Statistics, Certificate of Death 1927 #583.)*

ABERCRUMBIE, Tom
Owings, Laurens County
Laborer on sea coast fortifications
Served more than six months
Applied 19 April 1923; approved 20 April 1923
Affidavit: R. J. Stoddard and J. A. Putnam
Application #6943

ABRAHAM, Needham
Bishopville, Lee County
Laborer under Capt. Hutson
Served 1862–1863
Applied 7 May 1923; approved 24 May 1923
Affidavit: Henry Williams and Oliver Solomon
Application #7405: Needam Abraham, married, 82 years old, died 15 February 1925 in Lee County. Abraham was a farmer. *(SC Bureau of Vital Statistics, Certificate of Death 1924 #2823.)*

ADAIR, Alford
Renno, Laurens County
Cook under J. W., I. W., and Edmond Adair, Capt. B. S. Jones, Co. I, 3rd Regt
Served 1861 until close of war
Applied 20 April 1923; approved 21 April 1923
Affidavit: R. P. Adair, Sr., and T. F. Milam
Application #6944

ALBERT, Henry
Bishopville, Lee County

Laborer, Castle Pinckney breastworks under Capt. Devereaux
Served 1864–1865
Applied 24 April 1923; approved 24 May 1923
Affidavit: R. H. Scarbrough and R. M. Scarbrough
Application #7406

ALFRED, T. M.
McCormick, McCormick County
Servant under Capt. Jack Burris, Co. K, 7th Regt
Served October 1861–September 1863
Applied 28 April 1923; approved 15 May 1923
Affidavit: William Hufeldell, Sr., and W. E. Sheppard
Application #8120

ALLSTON, Jim
Cain Hoy, Charleston County
Camp attendant under Col. H. M. Rutledge, 25th NC Regt
Served 1861–end of the war
Applied 27 February 1928; approved 28 February 1928
Affidavit: Thomas P. Rutledge said Allston served under his father Col. Rutledge
Application #1736

Confederate leaders impressed African Americans across South Carolina to construct entrenchments on the South Carolina coast. Library of Congress.

ANDERSON, Burkett
Dunbarton, Barnwell County
Cook under G. W. Anderson, Capt. Geo. W. Stallings, Co. G, 2nd Art
Served September 1862–26 April 1865
Applied 26 April 1923; approved 30 April 1923
Affidavit: J. Staff Halford and J. A. Meyer
Application #1315

ANDERSON, David
Laurens, Laurens County
Laborer under Capt. Lipscomb on seacoast and island fortifications
Served more than a year during the war
Applied 21 April 1923; approved 21 April 1923
Affidavit: John N. Wright and L. S. Fuller
Application #6952

ANDERSON, George
Waterloo, Laurens County
Laborer on sea coast fortifications
Served more than twelve months
Applied 20 April 1923; approved 21 April 1923
Affidavit: J. C. Sims and A. W. Sims
Application #6953

ANDERSON, U. A.
Laurens, Laurens County
Laborer under Charles Simmons, overseer, seacoast and island fortifications
Served over six months
Applied 26 April 1923; approved 1 May 1923
Affidavit: J. M. Wright and Harry Davis
Application #6956

ARCH, Tom
Woodruff, Spartanburg County
Private, Capt. Nesbitt, Co. B, 1st Regt Cav
Served June 1861–April 1965
Applied 9 April 1923; approved 9 April 1923
Affidavit: J. W. Westmoreland and A. D. Chamblin
Application #10519

ASHFORD, James
Columbia, Richland County

Cook under Capt. Irby, Co. G, 7th Btn
Served April 1862–surrender 1865
Applied 14 May 1923; approved 16 May 1923
Affidavit: T. D. Ruff
Application #9852

B

BALDRIC, Abraham
Parler, Orangeburg County
Cook under Rufus Whitmore, Capt. Rufus LeGree, 2nd Art Regt
Applied 14 April 1924; approved 16 May 1924
Affidavit: L. F. Shuler and J. W. Livingston
Application #9183: Abraham Balderick, a widower, died 25 November 1925 when he was about 77 years old. He was born in Orangeburg County, and his father was Isaac Buldock. Balderick was buried at Portersville Church. Informant—Elmore Williams, Porter, SC *(SC Bureau of Vital Statistics, Certificate of Death, 1925 #19366)*

BARFIELD, J. B.
Bonneau, Berkeley County
Servant under Sgt. Joseph Harvey, Capt. Bartley
Applied 27 April 1923; approved 30 April 1923
Affidavit: Miss Sallie Harvey said Barfield served under Capt. Bartley
Application #1574: Jacob Barfield, 85 years, 11 months, and 3 days old, died in Berkeley County on 2 January 1927. A farmer, he was born in Berkeley County 3 January 1844 to Sallie Butler and Philip Barfield. On 4 January 1927 he was buried on the Dubose Plantation. Informant—Julius Lambright, Bonneau, SC *(SC Bureau of Vital Statistics, Certificate of Death, 1927 #168)*

BARKSDALE, Wash
Barksdale, Laurens County
Cook and attendant under Thomas Barksdale, Capt. R. P. Todd, Co. G, 3rd Regt, SC Inf
Served 14 April 1861–20 September 1862 when "Thomas Barksdale was killed at Chickamauga."
Applied 19 April 1923; approved 10 April 1923
Affidavit: T. Y. Henderson and Mel Fleming
Application #6981

BARRETT, Emmett
Aiken, Aiken County
Cook under John E. Gardner, Capt. William Hutto, Co. C, 8th Regt
Served 13 July 1864–9 April 1865
Applied 19 April 1923; approved 15 May 1923
Affidavit: John E. Gardner
Application #252: Emmett Barrett, a widower, 84 years old, died in Aiken County on 27 March 1931. He was a gardener, and his parents were George and Sylvia Barrett. He was buried on 30 March 1931 in Aiken. Informant—Sylvia Barrett, Aiken, SC *(SC Bureau of Vital Statistics, Certificate of Death, 1931 #3329)*

BAXTER, Charles
Rowesville, Orangeburg County
Cook under Dr. Andrew F. Crum, 21st SC Regt
Served with Dr. Crum near Charleston, SC and in Virginia for over three years
Baxter said he was over eighty years old on 14 April 1923 and had belonged to the Rev. Mr. L. J. Crum during slavery.
Affidavit: B. S. Crum said the Rev. Mr. L. J. Crum was his father and Dr. Andrew F. Crum was his brother. L. C. Boone said the Rev. Mr. L. J. Crum was his grandfather, and Dr. Andrew Crum was his uncle. Neither L. J. nor Andrew Crum were living in 1923.
Application #9187

BING, Tom
Furman, Hampton County
"Private soulder," Capt. Bill Peeples, Colcock Regt
Served fall 1861 until "I was mustered out in 1865"
Applied 21 April 1923; approved 28 April 1923
Affidavit: J. D. Goethe and L. Mixon
Application #6082: Tom Bing, a widower, died 28 January 1927 in Hampton County. The son of Matthew Bing and Annie Dore Williams, Bing was a farmer and 111 years old at his death. On 29 January 1927, Bing was buried at Thankful Church. Informant—John Bing, Furman, SC *(SC Bureau of Vital Statistics, Certificate of Death, 1927 #795.*

BIVINGS, Patrick
Greer, Spartanburg County
Cook under Ed Bivings
Served about a year
Applied 28 April 1923; approved 24 May 1923
Affidavit: Thomas Jefferson Burnett and William Columbus Hadden
Application #10557

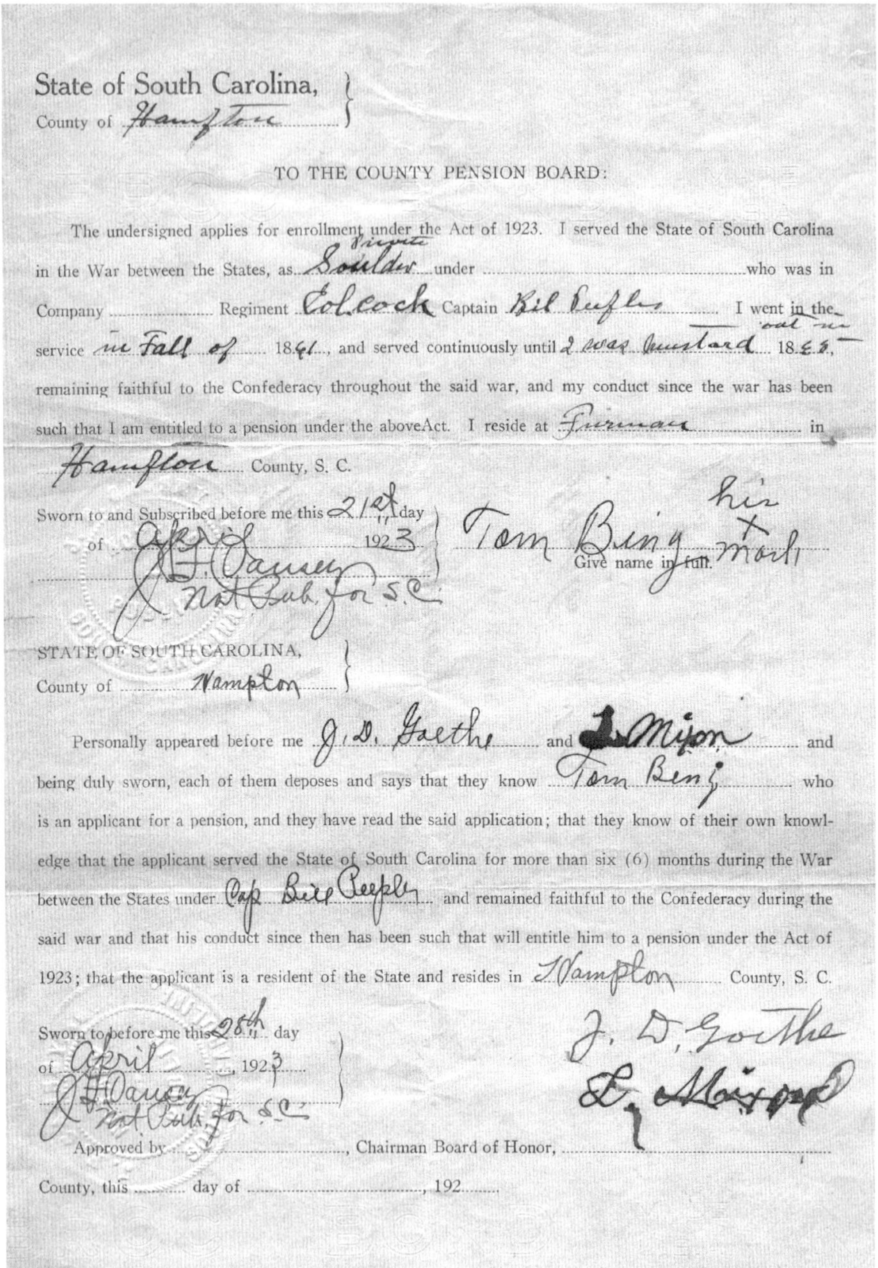

State of South Carolina,
County of Hampton

TO THE COUNTY PENSION BOARD:

The undersigned applies for enrollment under the Act of 1923. I served the State of South Carolina in the War between the States, as Private Soulder under .... who was in Company .... Regiment Colcock Captain Bil Peeples I went in the service in Fall of 1861, and served continuously until I was mustard out in 1865, remaining faithful to the Confederacy throughout the said war, and my conduct since the war has been such that I am entitled to a pension under the above Act. I reside at Furman in Hampton County, S. C.

Sworn to and Subscribed before me this 21st day of April 1923
J. F. Dancey
Not. Pub. for S.C.

Tom Bing his X mark
Give name in full.

STATE OF SOUTH CAROLINA,
County of Hampton

Personally appeared before me J. D. Goethe and L. Mixon and being duly sworn, each of them deposes and says that they know Tom Bing who is an applicant for a pension, and they have read the said application; that they know of their own knowledge that the applicant served the State of South Carolina for more than six (6) months during the War between the States under Cap Bill Peeples and remained faithful to the Confederacy during the said war and that his conduct since then has been such that will entitle him to a pension under the Act of 1923; that the applicant is a resident of the State and resides in Hampton County, S. C.

Sworn to before me this 28th day of April, 1923
J. F. Dancey
Not. Pub. for S.C.

J. D. Goethe
L. Mixon

Approved by ...., Chairman Board of Honor, ...
County, this .... day of ...., 192........

Tom Bing's application to the Hampton County Pension Board. Records of the Comptroller General, Pension Applications, 1919–1926, #6082. South Carolina Department of Archives and History (SCDAH).

BLACK, Jeff
Abbeville, Abbeville County
Cook under Lewis Perrin, Capt. J. W. Perrin
Served 1863–end of war
Applied 5 May 1923 for service as a laborer. Clerk noted 27 May 1924 that "the amendment to the Act cuts out all Laborers and only covers those that went as Body Servants or Camp Cooks and were actually in the Army." Application amended and approved 28 May 1924
Application #16: Jefferson Black, a widower, died in Abbeville County on 18 August 1930. Born in 1845, Black, a day laborer, was 85 years old at his death. On 20 August 1930, he was buried at Campfield. Informant—Tena White, Abbeville, SC. *(SC Bureau of Vital Statistics, Certificate of Death 1930 #18123)*

***BLUME, Wash**
Near Orangeburg, Orangeburg County
Servant under John H. Livingston, Co. D 20th Regt, Capt. Dick Danelly
Served 1863–end of war
Applied 12 April 1923
Affidavit: Dr. Thomas A. Jones
Application #9192

BOLD, Sam
Beaufort, Beaufort County
Servant of M. Jenkins, Capt. H. M. Stuart, Beaufort Volunteer Artillery
Served 1861–1865
Approved 1 February 1924
Affidavit: H. M. Stuart said that to the "best of his knowledge and belief" Sam Bold served under "his master." Affidavit of Ben Singleton says Bold was a servant of Michael Jenkins.
Application #1520

BOULWARE, Ed
Rt 2 Leeds, Fairfield County
Cook and laundryman under Pink Boulware, Co. B, 17th Regt
Applied 17 April 1923; approved 21 April 1923
Affidavit: T. E. Dye and M. (Mell) P. Dickerson
Application #3672

BOWIE, Jefferson
Bradley, Greenwood County
Servant under J. W. Bush, Co. B, 7th Regt
Served 1861–1865

Applied 27 April 1923
Affidavit: F. B. Rush
Application #5824: Jeff Bowie, married, 90 years old, died 16 November 1927 in Greenwood County. He was a retired farmer, his mother was Hannah Richey. On 20 November 1927, he was buried at Old Field Bethel. Informant—Sophie Rapley, Bradley, RFD, SC *(SC Bureau of Vital Statistics, Certificate of Death 1927 #18494)*

BOYD, Richard Sidney
Peak, Richland County
Laborer under Col. Davis, who was in "command of the labor forces"
Served seven weeks in 1861, came home; returned in 1862, worked four weeks, and also served two other terms of four weeks.
Applied 28 April 1923; approved 1 May 1923
Affidavit: J. K. Summer and C. M. Stuck
Application #9885: Richard Boyd, a married farmer, died 26 July 1924 in Richland County. Born 25 October 1844, his parents were Janie and Morris Boyd. Boyd was buried 26 July 1924 at Pinegrove. Informant—Morris Boyd, Peak, SC *(SC Bureau of Vital Statistics, Certificate of Death 1924 #13603)*

BOYKIN, William
Camden, Kershaw County
Body servant under Dr. Thomas Boykin, Capt. Goldsby, 10th Alabama Cav
Served 1861–surrender in 1865
Applied 20 April 1923; approved 7 May 1923
Affidavit: H. R. Boykin said William Boykin served "under Capt. Goldsby, 10th Alabama Cav and under Gen James Cantey." Hunter R. Boykin also said William Boykin was body servant to Dr. Tom Boykin of Portland, Alabama. After two years with the Western Army, Dr. Boykin transferred to Gen. James Cantey's brigade. Gen. Wilson's union troops captured Dr. Boykin and William Boykin during the battle of Selma, Alabama. William Boykin was assigned to a Union colonel, who gave him fifty dollars in gold. William Boykin then escaped by swimming the Alabama River and returned to his home. He shared the gold with his destitute mistress.
Application #6572: William Boykin, a widowed farmer, 97 years old, died 19 June 1924 in Kershaw County. On 20 June 1924 he was buried in Camden, SC. Informant—William Boykin, Jr., Camden, SC. *(SC Bureau of Vital Statistics, Certificate of Death 1924 #11031)*

BRABHAM, Ervin
Olar, Bamberg County
Servant under Capt. J. F. Brabham, Co. C, 1st SC Regt

Served 1863–1865
Applied 25 May 1923; approved 25 May 1923
Affidavit: J. B. Kearse and J. S. Breland
Application # 1176

BRANNON, John
Columbia, Richland County
Laborer under Jim Cromer "in charge of works"
Served 1862–April 12, 1865
Applied 11 April 1923; approved 11 April 1923
Affidavit: E. A. Lorick and Paul Wingard
Application #9890

BRISTER, Commedore
Barnwell, Barnwell County
Cook under Elonzo Ashley, Capt. W. B. Peeples, Co. K, 3rd Regt
Served March 1862–April 1865
Applied 12 April 1923; approved 16 April 1923
Affidavit: G. P. Morris and J. Staff Halford
Application #1335: Commodore Bristow, a widower and retired well digger, died in Barnwell County on 10 July 1933. Aged 85 years old at his death, Bristow was buried 11 July 1933 in Wilson Cemetery. *(SC Bureau of Vital Statistics, Certificate of Death, 1933 #9365)*

BROWN, Andrew
Blackville, Barnwell County
Cook under J. E. Templeton, Capt. J. W. Lancaster, Co. B, 2nd Regt
Served 1863–end of the war
Applied 5 May 1923; approved 21 May 1923
Affidavit: W. B. Carroll and F. W. Boylston
Application #1336

BROWN, Green
Woodruff, Spartanburg County
Cook under Capt. Willis, 18th Regt
Served fall 1861–1865
Applied 29 September 1923; approved 14 June 1924
Affidavit: D. Z. Mabry regarding Green Brown's service under Col. Jenkins
Application #10575

BROWN, Nelson
McCormick, McCormick County
Cook under John F. and Ed Calhoun, Capt. P. H. Bradley, Co. C, 7th Regt

Served May 1861–May 1862
Applied 7 May 1923; approved 7 May 1923
Affidavit: S. S. McBride and John B. Harmon
Application #8131

BROWN, Zack
Woodward, Fairfield County
Body servant under Capt. Robert F. Coleman, Co. B, 4th SC Cav
Served 1862–1864. Brown said he did not know the exact dates, but he "was with Robt F Cameron [sic] until he was wounded, stayed with him in hospital 'til it was captured."
Applied 20 April 1923; approved 28 April 1923
Affidavit: T. E. Dye and M. P. Dickerson
***Application #3680*:** Zack Brown, a married farmer and preacher, died in Fairfield County on 1 June 1934. Born in 1847, he was 87 years old at his death. His mother was Martha Weaver. On 2 June 1934 he was buried at Sweet Prospect. Informant—William Brown, Woodward, SC. *(SC Bureau of Vital Statistics, Certificate of Death, 1934 #8924)*

BUGG, Jim
Abbeville, Abbeville County
Cook under George Patterson, Co. A, 3rd Regt, SC Cav
Served 1862–April 1865
Applied 21 April 1923; approved 21 April 1923
Affidavit: J. H. [Drennlost]
***Application #31*:** James Bugg, married to Frances Bugg, died in Abbeville County on 21 January 1934. He was 87 years old when he died, and he was the son of Pricilla Merion and Matthew Buggs. On 23 January 1934 he was buried at Little Mountain. Informant—Frances Buggs, Abbeville RFD. *(SC Bureau of Vital Statistics, Certificate of Death, 1934 #1394)*

BUNCH, Joseph
Holly Hill, Orangeburg County
Cook under A. A. Way, CSA
Served 1 May 1864–end of the war
Applied 30 April 1923; approved 24 May 1923
Affidavit: James A. Stoutamire and Rachel M. Way Stoutamire. Rachel Stoutamire said Joseph Bunch was a slave of her father, A. A. Way, and that he was born 10 July four years before she was. She said she would be 74 years old on 2 July 1923. Her father took Joseph Bunch into service with him for six months and then sent Bunch home to stay with his sons A. C. and W. D. Way. A. A. Way then took Simon, Joseph's brother, into service with him.

Application #9211: Joseph Bunch, a widowed carpenter, died in Orangeburg County on 11 May 1924. When he died, he was 80 years old. Bunch was the son of Nancy Way and William Bunch. On 12 May 1924 he was buried at Tauget A. M. E. Church. Informant—J. A. Smith, Holly Hill, SC. *(SC Bureau of Vital Statistics, Certificate of Death, 1924 #9084)*

***BURGESS, William Thomas**
Elloree, Orangeburg County
Servant under Frank Moon, 3rd SC Regt, Capt. Tom Maffet
Served 1864
Applied 17 May 1923; approved 16 May 1923
Affidavit: Walter I. Herbert
Application #9214

BURNSIDE, Sam
Laurens, Laurens County
Laborer, coastal fortifications
Served 1863–1864
Applied 14 April 1923; approved 19 April 1923
Affidavit: Mrs. Jane Barksdale and Corrie L. Kennedy
Application #7012

BURTON, James (formerly Larkin Burton)
Wagener, Aiken County
Servant and cook under Henry Seigler, Capt. A. Morgan, Co. A, Hampton's Legion, Lt. Art
Served February 1862–October 1864
Applied 22 August 1923; approved 7 February 1924
Affidavit: Mrs. Kathryn Seigler Hughey and W. M. Seigler. Mrs. Hughey and W. M. Seigler said Larkin Burton was born 15 September 1840 and served with his master Henry Seigler. T. P. Morgan said Henry Seigler, Sandy Seigler, and Greggs Seigler were in his father's company.
Application #1523

BUSH, Aderson
Williston, Barnwell County
Laborer under Hatcher in Charleston on the Battery and Building Bomb Troop
Served at Charleston 1863–1865
Applied 28 May 1923
Affidavit: M. P. Hutson and Glosten Phlem
Application #1339

BUTLER, Ed
South Greenwood, Greenwood County
Servant under Frank R. Lipscomb and orderly for Gen. M. C. Butler
Served 1864–1865
Applied 16 April 1923
Affidavit: J. R. Irwin "believes" that Butler was a "servant of Frank Lipscomb."
Application #5844: Ed Butler, married, died in Greenwood County on 20 November 1923. He was retired, and he was the son of Annie and Jim Butler. He was buried on 21 November 1923 at Dysons, SC. Informant—Seymour Butler, Greenwood, SC. (SC Bureau of Vital Statistics, Certificate of Death, 1923 #17625)

BYRD, Cain
RFD #2 Edgefield, Edgefield County
Servant under Capt Hobson Byrd, Co. K, 15th SC Regt
Served December 1863–end of the war
Applied 11 April 1923; approved 26 May 1923.

African Americans served as stevedores, pilots, and in other maritime occupations. Library of Congress.

Affidavit: William B. Byrd and J. S. Byrd. M. B. Byrd said Cain Byrd served eighteen months.
Application # 3482

C

CAMPBELL, Paul
James Island, Charleston County
Body Servant under Lt. W. G. Hinson, Co. G, 7th Regt, SC Cav, Capt. W. H. Jefford
Served until April 1865
Applied 29 March 1924; approved 4 April 1924
Affidavit: W. A. Clark
Application #1773: Paul Campbell, widowed, farmer, died in Charleston County on 13 May 1934. Born in 1840, Campbell was 94 years old when he died. His wife was Maria Campbell. He was buried on 15 May 1934 on James Island, SC. Informant—William Mikell, James Island, SC. *(SC Bureau of Vital Statistics, Certificate of Death, 1934 #6974)*

CANNON, Josh
Newberry, Newberry County
Cook under Henry Stone, Co. F, 20th Regt, SCV, Capt. John M. Kinard
Served 1864–April 1865
Applied 14 April 1923; approved 23 April 1923
Affidavits: J. C. Wilson and William Y. Fair
Application #8441

CANNON, L. G. W.
Laurens, Laurens County
Laborer, fortifications, seacoast and islands
Served more than six months
Applied 23 April 1923; approved 8 May 1923
Affidavits: P. D. Metts and D. G. Long
Application #7019

CANNON, Press
Newberry, Newberry County
Cook under Bill Stone, 20th Regt., SCV, Capt. E. S. Keitt

Served 1861–April 1865
Applied 14 April 1923; approved 23 April 1923
Affidavits: J. C. Wilson and William Y. Fair
Application #8442

CARMICHAEL, Elijah
At Miss Mary Carmichael's, Dillon County
Cook under A. B. Carmichael, Co. L, 21st Regt, Capt. H. Legette
Served March 1862–December 1862
Applied 12 May 1923; approved 12 May 1923
Affidavits: A. B. Carmichael and J. W. Turbeville
Application #3187

CASEY, Scipio
71 Kracke Street, Charleston, Charleston County
Body servant under Charles Snowden of Blue Hole Plantation
Applied 31 March 1923; approved 31 March 1923
Affidavits: Samuel Faber and Mrs. S. G. Stoney
Application #1776: Scipio Casey, widower, 74 years old, died in Charleston County on 26 August 1925. The son of John Casey, he was buried on 28 August 1925 at Morris Street Baptist. Informant—Saddie Weathers, Charleston, SC. *(SC Bureau of Vital Statistics, Certificate of Death 1925 #3828)*

CHAPMAN, General
Irmo, Richland County
Cook and servant under Capt. George Haltiwanger, 3rd Regt
Served 1861–1865
Applied 28 April 1923; approved 8 May 1923
Affidavit: J. L. Haltiwanger
Application #9913: General Chapman, tenant farmer, died 11 February 1934 in Newberry County. His wife was Isabella Chapman. He was 93 years old when he died. He was the son of Pricey Chapman. On 12 February 1934, he was buried at Little Mountain cemetery. Informant—Almina Sligh. *(SC Bureau of Vital Statistics, Certificate of Death, 1934 #2521)*

CHAPPELL, Ben
Greenwood, Greenwood County
Servant under Milton Coleman, Co. B
Served January 1862–April 1865
Applied 14 April 1923
Affidavit: E. W. Creswell
Application #5849: Ben Chappell, Sr., died 12 September 1928 in Greenwood

County. Chappell, born 1830, was 98 years old at his death. A retired widower, he was the son of Henry and Charity Chappell and buried 16 September 1928 at Ninety-Six, SC. Informant—Ben Chappell, Jr., Ninety-Six, SC. *(SC Bureau of Vital Statistics, Certificate of Death 1928 #16414)*

***CHARLES, Jesse**
Near Manning, Clarendon County
Servant under William R. Coskrey, Co. I, 23rd Regt SCV, Capt. H. H. Lesesne
Served April 1861–April 1865
Applied 19 April 1923; approved 27 April 1923
Affidavits: S. Y. Barnes and I. N. Tobias
Application #2765

CHAVIS, Ransom
Eastover, Richland County
Cook under Capt. Meighan, Co. C, 2nd SC Cav
Served 1861–1865
Applied 7 May 1923; approved 16 May 1923
Affidavit: Mrs. M. A. Daly said he served under Myer Meighan
Application #9915: Ransom Chavis, widowed, died 7 April 1926 in Richland County. Chavis, a farmer, was born 1 March 1845, the son of John Chavis and Susan Berket. On 11 April 1926 he was buried at Dabner Pond Church. *(SC Bureau of Vital Statistics, Certificate of Death, 1926 #7356)*

***CHERRY, J. E.**
Seneca, Oconee County
Co. D. Orrs Regt, Capt. F. E. Harrison
Applied 20 April 1923; approved 20 April 1923
Affidavits: J. C. Cannon and W. T. McGill
Application #8910

CHILDS, Wade
Anderson, Anderson County
Servant under J. C. Chiles, Dr. T. C. Chiles and J. S. Chiles, Co. B, Orrs Rifles, Capt. J. S. Cothan
Served 1862– surrender 1865
Applied 6 April 1923; approved 12 April 1923
Affidavits: R. F. Driver and J. B. Lewis; M. L. Bonham said he had known Wade Chile for more than twenty years and remembered Col. Cothran saying Chiles had carried the wounded Cothran from the "field of battle at Second Manassas."
Application #734

M. L. BONHAM THOS. ALLEN

BONHAM & ALLEN
ATTORNEYS AT LAW
ANDERSON, SO. CAR.

April 6, 1923.

Hon. Herman E. Bailey,
Probate Judge,
City.

Dear Sir:-

I am taking the liberty to send to you the application for pension made by old Wade Chiles under the new act. The negro is old and his memory is infirm and he cannot remember anybody now living who can swear to his service. I am sending you my affidavit, which it seems to me should be sufficient to establish his service, because when he told me he carried Colonel Cothran off the field at Second Manassas, he did not know that I had heard Colonel Cothran years before state the same fact. I am afraid that the Board of Pensions are disposed to be a little technical in passing upon these applications.

Please do what you can for old Wade in the matter. He is a deserving old negro.

Yours very truly,

M L Bonham

MLB:M

Letter from former S. C. Governor M. L. Bonham regarding Wade Childs. Records of the Comptroller General, Pension Applications, 1919–1926, #734. SCDAH.

CLARY, Santaanna
Silverstreet, Saluda County
Cook under Wells Clary, Capt. Ham Brooks, Co. G, 7th Regt
Served Sept 1861–November 1863
Applied 13 April 1923; approved 21 May 1923
Affidavit: D. T. Crouch and Russell Wright
Application #10328: Santy Clary, a married farmer, died 16 May 1926. Born 12 October 1842, he was 84 years 7 months and 4 days old at his death. His parents were Sarah Moore and Santa Clary. On 11 May 1926 he was buried at Wesley Zion Cemetery. Informant—Gus Clary, Saluda, Rt. 2, SC. *(SC Bureau of Vital Statistics, Certificate of Death, 1926 #11543)*

***CLYBURN, Sam, Sr.**
Manning, Clarendon County
Servant under Lt. T. J. Clyburn, Co. G, 2nd SC Regt, Capt. C. C. Hail
Served April 1861–1865
Applied 21 April 1923; approved 21 April 1923
Affidavits: L. L. Clyburn and S. J. Benton
Application #2766

COHEN, Abram
Greenwood, Greenwood County
Servant under Capt. Hughet
Served 1864–1865
Applied 16 April 1923
Affidavit: W. H. Mays
Application #5856

COLEMAN, William P.
Leeds, Fairfield County
Cook and laundryman under W. P. Coleman, Co. A, 71st Regt, Capt. John McLurkin
Served fall 1863 for six months
Applied 17 April 1923; approved 28 April 1923
Affidavits: B. E. Lyles and Leroy Fee
Application #3690

COLLINS, Jim
Mt. Pleasant, Charleston County
Cook under Capt. Cornelius Sams, Capt. Elias Venning
Served 1863–1865
Applied 24 September 1923; approved 24 March 1924

Affidavits: Mrs. J. Rutledge Smith and Mrs. Nancy Scott
Application #1780

COOPER, Amos
Oceda, Georgetown County
Cook under H. J. Bailey, Jr., German Artillery, Capt. Melcher
Served January 1864–April 1865
Applied 21 April 1923
Affidavits: J. C. Bailey and R. W. Bailey
Application #4050: Amos Cooper, widower, between 85 and 90 years old, died in Georgetown County on 7 June 1925. He was the son of Celia Wright and Harry Cooper. He was buried 8 June 1921 at St. Mary's. Informant—R. W. Bailey. Bailey noted that Cooper was "one of my father's old slaves, served my brother as Cook etc. during the war between The States. A faithful servant gone to his reward." *(SC Bureau of Vital Statistics, Certificate of Death, 1925 #9868)*

***COOPER, Daniel**
Sumter County
Servant under Lt. W. A. Cooper, Browns Btn Reserves guarding prisoners at Florence, SC
Source: List submitted by Thomas E. Richardson, judge of probate, Sumter County, 13 June 1923
Application #11276b

COPELAND, Spencer (two applications)
1. Clinton, Laurens County
Laborer under John Sullivan, Co. A, 3rd Regt, Capt. Garlington
Served 1861–1862
Applied 3 May 1923; approved 9 May 1923
Affidavits: D. E. Tribble and R. P. Adair
Application #7314: Note on back says this 1923 application of Spencer Copeland was mistakenly enrolled for John Sullivan. The chairman of the county board discovered the mistake and paid Copeland seven dollars which was "held over" from 1923. Copeland submitted another application in 1924, but was no longer eligible.
2. Clinton, Laurens County
Laborer at Charleston breastworks under John Sullivan, Co. A, 3rd Regt, SC Inf
Served about six months; injured foot while spading barefoot and later had leg amputated
Applied 8 March 1924; disapproved 8 March 1924
Affidavits: R. J. Copeland, Sr., Co. E, 4 Batn State Troops and R. P. Adair, Sr., Co. A, 13 Regt, SCV

Application #7040: Spencer Copeland, widowed, farmer, died 9 May 1931 in Laurens County. His wife was Emma Copeland. About 90 years old when he died, Copeland was the son of Frances and Henry Copeland. He was buried 10 May 1931 at Bethel. Informant—Lewis Copeland, Clinton, SC. *(SC Bureau of Vital Statistics, Certificate of Death, 1931 #8178)*

***CRAWFORD, Sanders**
Abbeville County
Servant to an uncle of Pearl M. Beckwith
Source: Letter from Beckwith to chief clerk of the pension board, 11 July 1924. Clerk said the roll for 1924 was closed. Items # 232 and 233

CRAYTON, Jake
Walhalla, Oconee County
Servant under Lt. Gus Lewis, Co. K, Orrs Rifles, Capt. Cheshire
Served Petersburg, Virginia 1864–surrender 1865
Applied 5 May 1923
Affidavits: W. T. McGill and J. W. Cannon
Application #8925: Jake Crayton, widowed, fish merchant, died in Oconee County on 17 December 1930. About 75 years old when he died, Crayton was buried 18 December 1930 at Flat Rock. Informant—Allen Crayton, Walhalla, SC. *(SC Bureau of Vital Statistics, Certificate of Death, 1930 #21406.)*

CROSS, Council
Williston, Barnwell County
Cook under R. W. McCreary, Colcock's Regt, Capt. P. M. Wills
Served 1 November 1860–29 May 1865
Applied 23 May 1923; approved 24 May 1923
Affidavits: R. W. McCreary and J. A. M. Gardner
Application #1358: Council C. Cross, widowed and retired, died 25 November 1923. He was 73 years old, the son of Emlie McCreary and Arnold Cross, and was buried 16 November 1923 in Goose Pond Cemetery. Informant—John Harris, Williston, SC. *(SC Bureau of Vital Statistics, Certificate of Death, 1923 #16989.)*

D

DANIELS, Marcus
Hilda, Barnwell County
Cook under Capt. H. Ray, Co. H, 17th Regt
Served 1861–September 1862

Applied 8 May 1923; approved 8 May 1923
Affidavits: Starling Hutto and H. J. Croft
Application #1359

DARBY, Jim
Fort Motte, Calhoun County
Servant under Capt. Trezevant, Blacks Regt
Served fall 1861–1865
Applied 1 May 1923; approved 7 May 1923
Affidavits: B. R. Griffith and B. Walling
Application #1691: Jim Darby died 3 December 1927 in Calhoun County. The son of John Darby, he was buried at Darby on 4 December 1927. Informant—Dave Darby, St. Matthews, SC. *(SC Bureau of Vital Statistics, Certificate of Death, 1927 #19676.)*

DARBY, Newton
Prosperity, Newberry County
Cook under Henry Simms Co. A, 4th Btn, Capt. H. C. Mosely
Served January 1864–April 1865
Applied 23 April 1923; approved 8 May 1923
Affidavits: J. C. Counts and G. P. Werts
Application #8459: Newton Darby, 80 years old, a widowed farmer, died 4 July 1928 in Newberry County. The son of Polly Ann and Nathan Darby, he was buried 5 July 1924 at Shiloh. Informant—Ora Moseley, Prosperity, SC. *(SC Bureau of Vital Statistics, Certificate of Death, 1928 #13354.)*

DATT, Lazarus
Estill, Hampton County
Servant under Elliott Solomons, 3rd SC Cav, Capt. Alfred Martin
Served 1861–April 1865
Applied 4 February 1923; approved 5 February 1923
Affidavits: H. L. Solomons and J. L. Morrison
Application #6106

DAVIS, Harry
Laurens, Laurens County
Laborer under Charles Simmons on fortifications, seacoast and islands
Served 1861–1865
Applied 26 April 1923; approved 1 May 1923
Affidavits: J. N. Wright and M. A. Anderson
Application #7050

DAVIS, Henry
Blair, Fairfield County
Cook and servant under J. W. Lyles, Co. K, 1st Regt, SC Cav, Capt. A. P. Brown
Served September 1863–May 1864
Applied 26 April 1923; approved 28 April 1923
Affidavits: John W. Lyers and Jas H. Timmons (2)
Application #3692

DAVIS, Isham
Rt 3, Campobello, Spartanburg County
Servant under Lt. John Bankston Davis, Capt. Buck Bishop, Co. I, Holcombe Legion
Served Jan 1861–fall 1861
Applied 14 April 1923; approved 14 June 1924
Affidavit: N. A. Wallace and B. W. Shurburt
Application #10662: Isom Davis, 85 years old, died 11 September 1928 in Spartanburg County. A farmer, he was the son of John Abbot and Provy. Davis was buried 13 September 1928 at Pleasant Grove. Informant—Fred Bell, Inman, SC. *(SC Bureau of Vital Statistics, Certificate of Death, 1928 #17041.)*

DAVIS, June
Early Branch, Hampton County
Cook under W. W. McTeer (his "young master"), 2nd SCV, Hampton's Legion, Capt. Tom Scriven
Served November 1861–1865
Applied 10 May 1923; approved 14 May 1923
No affidavit because "There are no living . . . personal eye witnesses."
Application #6108

***DAVIS, Nelson**
Greenville, Greenville County
Servant and cook under John C. and Robert C. Davis, 7th Cav
Affidavits: J. W. C. Bell and John C. Davis. Also, unsigned statement that Martin Wilson and Nelson Vance served in the cavalry. Nelson Vance was John C. Davis' servant, and Martin Wilson served with Wash Miller.
Application #11548d

***DAWKINS, Mallory**
Greenville County
Servant and cook under Capt. Bunyan Davis, Co. F, 15 SC, Kershaw's Brigade
Served two years
Source: Letter of Alester G. Furman, 7 April 1923
Application #5783

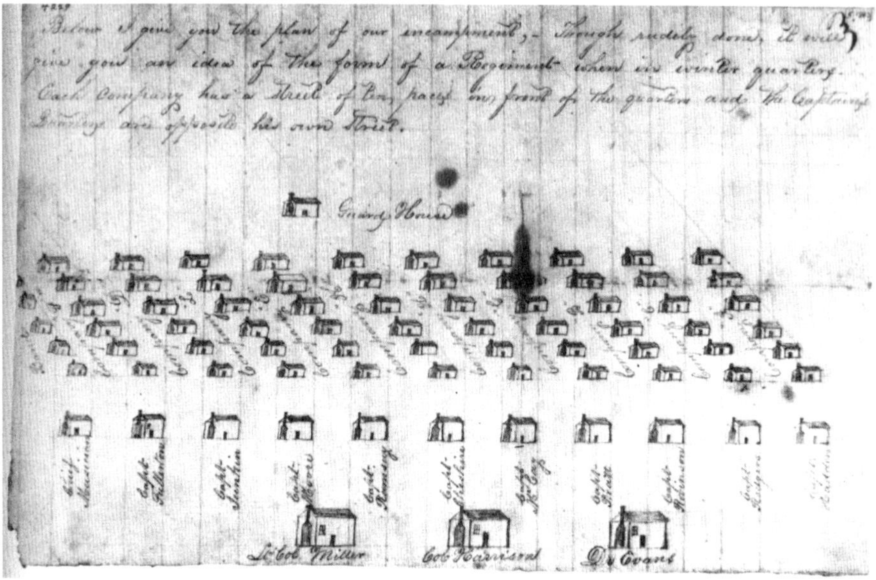

Sketch of winter camp, 1st South Carolina Rifles, Spotsylvania, Virginia, 1864. South Caroliniana Library. University of South Carolina.

DEAN, Aaron (Aron)
Pleasant Lane, Edgefield County
Cook under A. B. Dean, Co. K, 15th Regt, Capt. Hob Byrd
Served 1862–1864
Applied 18 May 1923; approved 26 May 1923
Affidavits: G. K. Timmerman and William E. Timmerman
Application #3509

DEAN, Elias
Greenwood, Greenwood County
Waitman under Jessie Wilbling, Hoods Co., Hawthorns Regt, Capt. Tom Denby
Served 1861–1865
Applied 7 April 1923
Affidavit: W. A. McLees
Application # 5877

DEAN, Henry
Wellford, Spartanburg County
Cook under Capt. George B. Dean, Co. E, SC Cav
Served summer 1864–the end of the war
Applied 30 April 1923; approved 24 May 1923

Affidavit: Mrs. A. E. Dean and J. Madison Dean. Accompanying letter from Alvin H. Dean said his "mother's information and belief" was that Henry Dean served with his uncle, George B. Dean, not his father. Dean's letter also said that an African American named Bob Dean accompanied his father, who was captain of Co. E, SC Cav. His uncle later became captain of the same company.
Application #10666: Henry Dean, widowed, farmer, died 15 January 1924 in Spartanburg County. Born 18 February 1843, he was the son of Kaline Dean and Henry Kilgo. Dean was buried 16 January 1924 at Florence Chapel. Informant—Will Dean, Wellford, SC. *(SC Bureau of Vital Statistics, Certificate of Death, 1924 #3351.)*

DELOACH, Richard
Cave, Allendale County
Cook under Sgt. Bower, Capt. Kirkland, Co. D, 3rd Regt
Served October 1861–April 1865
Applied 9 May 1923; approved 9 May 1923
Affidavits: J. W. Thomas and H. B. Carver
Application #574: Richard DeLoach, a widowed farm laborer, 84 years old, died 29 May 1926. He was the son of Harry and Livy DeLoach. He was buried in the DeLoach Cemetery. Informant—Cleo Dunbar, Allendale, SC. *(SC Bureau of Vital Statistics, Certificate of Death, 1926 #7796.)*

DENNIS, Jackson
Abbeville, Abbeville County
Cook under Brady, Capt. Robertson, Co. A, 15th Regt
Served 1862–end of war 1865
Applied 7 April 1923; approved 7 April 1923
Witnesses: Mrs. Fannie J. Marshall, J. S. Gilbert
Application #98

DESAUSSURE, Albert
Columbia, Richland County
Servant under Edgar and Eugene Clarkson, Capt. L. W. Taylor
Co. K, 3rd Regt
Served August 1864–April 12, 1865
Applied 18 April 1923; approved 16 April 1923
Affidavit: Mrs. J. Eugene Clarkson
Application #9950

DICKERSON, Robert
Blackville, Barnwell County
Cook under Capt. Joseph Dickerson, Co. G, 17th Regt
Served until war ended 1865

Applied 20 April 1923; approved 20 April 1923
Affidavits: C. H. Hartzog and Sterling Hutto
Application #1363

DONNELLY, Ben
Marion, Marion County
Cook, Co. C, 2nd Regt, SCV, Capt. W. F. Davis
Served November 1864–April 1865
Applied 12 May 1923; approved 26 May 1923
Affidavits: J. D. Montgomery
Application #7991

DRAKEFORD, Washington
Camden, Kershaw County
Cook under Capt. Joe Drakeford, Co. E, 2nd SC Regt
Served June 1862–1865
Applied 2 May 1923: approved 7 May 1923
Affidavits: Hiram Mitchel and H. Truesdale
Application #6597

DRAYTON, Cato L.
#91 St. Philip Street, Charleston, Charleston County
Cook under J. R. P. Ravenel, Parker's Battery, Marion Art, Capt. Ed L. Parker
Served March 1862–February 1865
Applied 9 April 1923; approved 9 April 1923
Affidavit: J. R. P. Ravenel
Application #1803

DRAYTON, Isaac
Charleston, Charleston County
Servant under Philip Pepper, Cav, Capt. Elias Venning
Served 1861–1864
Applied 16 April 1923; approved 16 April 1923
Affidavit: R. S. Venning
Application #1804: Isaac Drayton, a widowed porter, died 24 August 1931 in Charleston, SC. Born 10 April 1836, Drayton was 95 years 4 months and 14 days old at his death. He was buried at Zion Presbyterian Church. Informant—Ruth Palmer, 31 Morris Street, Charleston, SC. *(SC Bureau of Vital Statistics, Certificate of Death, 1931 #12930.)*

DRUMMOND, Milton
Spartanburg, Spartanburg County
Laborer under H. E. Drummond, Capt. George Dean, 2nd Regt

Served 1862–first of 1865
Applied 5 April 1923; approved 24 May 1923
Affidavit: J. W. Westmoreland and A. D. Chamblin
Application #10681: Milton Drummond, son of Julius (?) and Charlotte Drummond, died 22 April 1924. Born in 1834, Drummond was 79 years old and married. Informant—Jessie Drummond, 183 Stevens Street, Spartanburg, SC. *(SC Bureau of Vital Statistics, Certificate of Death, 1924 #7246.)*

DUNBAR, Boston
Meyers Mill (P. O. Williston), Barnwell County
Worker on the battery under George Black and Capt. Alexander Willingham
Served 1864–1865
Applied 15 May 1923; approved 21 May 1923
Affidavits: J. Staff Halford and J. A. Meyer
Application #1364

E

***EGLESTON, Sam**
Three miles from Winnsboro, Fairfield County
Waiter under J. W. Coleman, Co. C, 6th SC Cav, Capt. Goodwin, Col. Aiken's Regt, Butlers Brigade
Served November 1861–surrender 1865
Applied 29 February 1924; approved 22 April 1924
Affidavit: W. S. Robinson, who belonged to the same company as J. W. Coleman
Application #3702

***ELLERBE, Isaac**
Cheraw, Chesterfield County
Cook under Zach Ellerbe, 6th SC Regt
Served 1862–1864
Applied 29 May 1923; approved 31 May 1923
Affidavit: H. P. Duvall and M. W. Duvall
Application #2615b

ELLIOTT, Gas
Near Belvedere, Aiken County
Servant under Col. Dave Shaw, Capt. T. W. Whatley
Served fall 1862–April 9, 1865
Applied 30 April 1923; approved 23 April 1924

Affidavits: Botsford Green and C. M. Horne
Application #306

ELLIS, Calep
Bowman, Orangeburg County
Applied 29 January 1926
Affidavits: H. L. Cunch and M. M. Shot
Application #9269: Caleb Ellis was 96 years old when he died on 22 October 1934. He was married to Sarah Ann. The son of Pauline Ellis, he was buried at Target Church. Informant—Carrie Ellis, Holly Hill, SC. *(SC Bureau of Vital Statistics, Certificate of Death, 1934 #16336.)*

F

FINLEY, Amos
Brunson, Hampton County
Cook and servant under Augustus Finley, Co. E, 11th Regt, Capt. Mikler
Served 1863–surrender 1865
Applied 5 April 1923; approved 7 April 1923
Affidavit: Henry M. Preacher
Application #6118

FLOYD, Henry
Meyers Mill, Barnwell County
Servant under Capt. Henry Buist, Sharpshooters
Served 10 September 1861–Lee's surrender
Applied 14 April 1923; approved 25 April 1923
Affidavits: J. A. Meyer and J. Staff Halford
Application #1372: Henry Floyd, a married farmer, died at age 90 on 3 January 1927 in Barnwell County. The son of Simon Hankinson and Mary Floyd, he was buried at Indian Grove. Informant—Hosey Floyd, Meyer Mill, SC. *(SC Bureau of Vital Statistics, Certificate of Death, 1927 #141.)*

FOOTMAN, Josh
Harleyville, Dorchester County
Cook under Capt. John Sellers, Col. Olin Dantzler
Served 1862–1865
Applied 16 April 1923; approved 30 April 1923
Affidavit: R. D. Zimmerman
Application #3353: Joshua Footman, a widower, about 93 years old, died 24

August 1923 in Dorchester County. The son of Anthony and Amy Footman, he did odd jobs. Informant—(son) Footman, Harleyville. *(SC Bureau of Vital Statistics, Certificate of Death, 1923 #12795.)*

FORD, Edwin P.
Georgetown, Georgetown County
Cook and drummer under J. H. Read, Co. A, 21st Regt, Col. Graham, Gen. Harley
Served 1861 until mustered out at Appomatox, 1865
Applied 24 April 1923
Affidavits: C. L. Count and W. E. Sparkman
Application #4061

FORD, Frederick
P. O. Campfield c/o Wardell Raush, Black River, Georgetown County
Wagon driver and cook under Shackelford, Capt. Brown, Gen. Napier
Served "commencement" 1861–Lee's surrender 1865
Applied 1 May 1923
Affidavit: B. P. Fraser
Application #4062

FORD, Henry James
Plantersville, Georgetown County
Cook under Capt. John Tucker, Marions Men of Winyah
Served 1862–1865
Applied 23 April 1923; approved 14 May 1923
Affidavit: Benjamin P. Fraser
Application # 4063: Henry J. Ford, a married farmer, 94 years old, died 10 August 1926 in Georgetown County. The son of George Ford and Kay Furman, Ford was born 10 August 1832 and buried at St. Paul. Informant—Nasa Ford, Plantersville, SC. *(SC Bureau of Vital Statistics, Certificate of Death, 1926 #14729.)*

FOXWORTH, William
Marion RFD 2, Marion County
Laborer on Charleston breastworks under E. A. Coleman
Served part of 1863 and 1864
Applied 26 May 1923; approved 26 May 1923
Affidavit: J. D. Montgomery
Application #7999: William H. Foxworth, a married farmer, 80 years old, died 19 September 1924 in Marion County. The son of Plenty Foxworth and Rosa White, he was buried at Singletary Church. Informant—Meta Foxworth, Marion, SC. *(SC Bureau of Vital Statistics, Certificate of Death, 1924 #16856.)*

FRANKLIN, Trus
Marion RFD 4, B. 65, Marion County
Cook under B. Frank Davis, 10th Regt, SCV, Capt. Miller
Served 1861–August 1862 and later until 1863
Applied 26 May 1923; approved 26 May 1923
Application #8000

FRANKS, Ben
Fountain Inn, Laurens County
Cook and attendant under John M. Franks, Co. D, 3rd Btn, Capt. J. M. Gunels
Served March 1862–August 1863
Applied 12 April 1923; approved 12 April 1923
Affidavits: J. H. Franks and J. P. Caldwell
Application #7085: Benjamin Franks, a widowed farmer, 90 years old, died 20 February 1928 in Greenville County. He was buried at Bethlehem Church. Informant—Martha Sullivan, Simpsonville, SC. *(SC Bureau of Vital Statistics, Certificate of Death, 1928 #4590.)*

FRAZIER, Markus
Abbeville, Abbeville County
Attendant to Capt. James Frazier
Served 1863–surrender 1865
Applied 19 May 1923; approved 19 May 1923
Application #66: Marcus Frazier, a widower, 72 years old, died 7 July 1927 in Abbeville County. He was the son of Jim Frazier and Josephine White and was buried in Abbeville. Informant—Viola Cowans, Abbeville, SC. *(SC Bureau of Vital Statistics, Certificate of Death, 1927 #10433.)*

FULLER, Dan
Waterloo, Laurens County
Cook and attendant under Capt. James Hudgens, Williams Battalion
Applied 14 April 1923; approved 20 April 1923
Affidavits: O. A. Winn and W. W. Campbell
Application #7090: Dan Fuller, married, 95 years old, died 21 May 1923 in Laurens County. He was buried at Bethel. Informant—Will Fuller, Laurens, SC. *(SC Bureau of Vital Statistics, Certificate of Death, 1928 #7996.)*

FUNCHESS, July
Orangeburg, Orangeburg County
Servant under Col. D. R. Barton
Served 1864–close of war
Applied 14 April 1923; approved 18 April 1923

Affidavits: Mrs. Jerome N. McMichael and Jerome N. McMichael. The McMichaels said Funchess served with their grandfather, Col. D. R. Barton
Application #9293: July Funches, married, farmer, 82 years old, died 10 December 1924 in Orangeburg County. He was the son of Chas Funches and Rosa Glover and was buried at Jerusalem Church. Informant—Eugenia Funches, RFD Box 174, Orangeburg, SC. *(SC Bureau of Vital Statistics, Certificate of Death, 1924 #23073.)*

G

GAILLARD, Philip
Campfield, Georgetown County
Wagon driver under Capt. Manigault, 104th Regt
Served February 1861–February 1865
Applied 30 April 1923
Affidavit: B. P. Fraser
Application #4064

***GALLUCHAT, July**
Manning, Clarendon County
Laborer on the Charleston area fortifications; wounded at Fort Sumter, September 1863; left leg amputated below the knee, and left hand amputated about the "middle third of the forearm."
Applied 26 March 1889; approved 16 April 1889. Board found he was disabled from earning a living and was a "true Democrat." Earlier in 1882, July Galluchat had petitioned for the value of an artificial arm. W. W. Holladay, I. I. Broadway, and R. J. Holladay supported that application. Joseph Galluchat, attorney of Manning, submitted July Galluchat's claim. Source: *Pensions, 1888–1906; Applications for Artificial Limbs, 1880–1887, 73–419, 74–420.*

GANTT, Ed
Great Cypress, Barnwell County
Cook and work on battery under John Aaron, Capt. Black
Served 1863–April 1865
Applied 13 April 1923; approved 13 April 1923
Affidavits: J. A. Meyer and J. Staff Halford
Application #1373: Ed Gantt, a widowed farm laborer, died 8 July 1934 in Barnwell County. The son of April Gantt, he was 89 years, 1 month, and 1 day old. He was buried in his home cemetery. Informant—Francis Beck, Barnwell, SC. *(SC Bureau of Vital Statistics, Certificate of Death 1934 #11973.)*

Maintaining coastal fortifications under Federal bombardment was hazardous work. Inside Fort Sumter, 1864. Library of Congress.

GANTT, F. W.
Salley, Aiken County
Helper under Capt. Robinson, Co. A, 4th Regt
Served 14 February 1862–May 1865
Applied 29 May 1923; approved 2 June 1923
Affidavits: Jake Garett and Priscilla Gunter
Application #328: There is a death certificate for Fleming Gantt, who was born 3 January 1844 and died 11 August 1925 in Aiken County. This Gantt was buried in the Smeetenting Graveyard. Informant—Phillip Thompson, Salley, SC. *(SC Bureau of Vital Statistics, Certificate of Death, 1925 #18100.)*

GANTT, Jake
Wagener RFD, Aiken County
Laborer under Robert Estus, Co. B, 4th Regt, TN, Capt. Robertson
Served February 1864–April 1865
Applied 29 May 1923; approved 2 June 1923
Affidavits: F. W. Gantt and Priscilla Gunter
Application #329

GARNER, James
Richland County
Laborer
Served 1863
Applied 27 April 1923; approved 28 April 1923
Affidavit: C. E. Eager and Alex G. Clarkson said Garner served at Fort Sumter and lived in Eastover.
Application #9986

GASQUE, John
Sampit, Georgetown County
Cook under James Williams, Co. A, Capt. Albert Thomas, Gen. Mart Gary
Served April 1863–Appomattox 1865
Applied 17 April 1923
Affidavits: R. W. Bailey and W. L. Mercer
Application #4065: John Gasque, widowed, farmer, 80 years old, died 3 August 1924 in Georgetown County. He was the son of Joe and Katie Gasque. He was buried at St. Paul Sampit. Informant—Ella Alston, Georgetown, SC. *(SC Bureau of Vital Statistics, Certificate of Death 1924 #14214.)*

GETHERS, Sandy
Bennetts Springs, Barnwell County
Cook under Capt. Bacon, 2nd Art
Served 1862–April 1865
Applied 25 April 1923; approved 25 April 1923
Affidavits: J. A. Meyer and J. Staff Halford
Application #1375: Sandon Gathers, single, 87 years old, was born 11 September 1840 and died 11 September 1927. He was the son of Sus and Branly Gathers and was buried at Holly ?. Informant—Augustas Matthews, Gough, SC. *(SC Bureau of Vital Statistics, Certificate of Death, 1927 #21580.)*

GILES, James
133 Wentworth Street, Charleston, Charleston County
Cook under Townsend Mikell, Co. I, 3rd Regt, SC Cav, Capt. J. C. Seabrook

Served from commencement of war 1861–end of war 1865
Applied 9 April 1923; approved 24 April 1923
Affidavits: J. Jenkins Mikell and Townsend Mikell
Application #1816: James Giles, a widowed merchant, 79 years old, died in Charleston County on 9 March 1924. Born in 1845, he was the son of James Giles and buried at M? St. Baptist. Informant—Frank Giles, 20 Short Street, Charleston, SC. *(SC Bureau of Vital Statistics, Certificate of Death, 1924 #3957.)*

GINN, Ransom
Hampton, Hampton County
Cook and servant under Samuel J. Lewis, Kirks Squadron, Capt. Manning Kirk
Served 1862–Honey Hill Battle 1864
Applied 17 May 1923; approved 25 May 1923
No affidavit as all witnesses were deceased, but the board recommended Ginn for a pension because "the statements and facts in this case, by traditional testimonies, are conclusive and satisfactory . . . "
Application #6120: Ransom Ginn, widowed and about 100 years old, died 12 March 1932 in Hampton County. The son of Adam and Jane Rodd, Ginn was buried at Hickory Hill Cemetery. Informant—John Washington, Hampton, SC. *(SC Bureau of Vital Statistics, Certificate of Death 1932 #9034.)*

GLOVER, Frank
Vance, Orangeburg County
Servant under J. B. Connor, Fredericks Regt, Capt. Thomas Legare
Served January 1862–April 1865
Applied 27 July 1926
Affidavit: Joe Kiett
Application #9309: Frank Glover, a married farmer, 83 years old, died 20 March 1928 in Orangeburg County. The son of Maderson Glover, he was buried in Rockey Hill Cemetery. Informant—Robert Lincoln, Vance, SC. *(SC Bureau of Vital Statistics, Certificate of Death, 1928 #5174.)*

GOODING, Joe
Luray RFD, Allendale County
Servant under Maj. John J. Gooding, Co. G, 11th Regt
Served 1861–"war ended" 1865
Applied 4 June 1923; approved 11 June 1923
Affidavits: W. F. Dobson and Mrs. John J. Gooding
Application #577

GOODWIN, Kit
Woodlands, Richland County

Servant under Col. Frank Hampton, 2nd Cav
Served from 1861 until surrender 1865
Applied 5 April 1923; approved 7 April 1923
Affidavit: Frank Hampton
Application #9994: Kitt Goodwin, widowed, farmer, 96 years old, died 25 February 1926 in Richland County. He was buried in the Childs Graveyard. Informant—James Wills, Columbia, SC. *(SC Bureau of Vital Statistics, Certificate of Death, 1926 #3195.)*

GRANT, Alfred
Cross Hill, Laurens County
Laborer, government hospital, James Island
Served 1861–1865
Applied 8 May 1923; approved 14 May 1923
Affidavits: J. R. Wells and T. J. Cole
Application #7110

GRANT, Fred
Abbeville, Abbeville County
Attendant, Capt Glick
Served 1864–1865
Applied 8 May 1923; approved 8 May 1923
Application #72

GRANT, Wesley
Cross Hill, Laurens County
Laborer, fortifications, Charleston and adjacent islands
Served more than six months
Applied 19 April 1923; approved 8 May 1923
Affidavits: J. M. Goodman and B. Goodman
Application #7111: Wess Grant, widowed, 96 years old, died 21 June 1927 in Laurens County. The son of Bill and Jessie Grant, he was buried in the Trumpler Cemetery. Informant—Helery Bullock, Cross Hill, SC. *(SC Bureau of Vital Statistics, Certificate of Death, 1927 #9640.)*

GREEN, Jacob
Cheraw, Chesterfield County
Cook under Capt. Craig and Capt. Henry McIver, Co. A, 5th Regt, SC Cav. An annotation says Green belonged to William Benton and while serving with him, cooked for the company mess.
Served March 1862–May 1864
Applied 9 April 1923

African Americans served with Federal and Confederate medical teams. Federal Ambulance detachment, Petersburg, Va., 1864. Michigan Department of State Archives.

Affidavits: G. A. Malloy and J. A. McCreight
Application #2612: Jacob Green, widowed, farmer, 81 years old, died 11 October 1925 in Chesterfield County. The son of Juano Green, he was buried at Foundy Hill. Informant—Preston Green, Darlington, SC. *(SC Bureau of Vital Statistics, Certificate of Death, 1925 #16882.)*

GREEN, Richard
Woodruff, Spartanburg County
Servant under Gen. Jim Green, Co. K, 5th Regt
Served 1863 and later for a total of eighteen months
Applied 23 April 1923; approved 24 May 1923
Affidavits: W. B. Lawson and A. D. Chambliss
Application #10720: Richard Green, a married farmer, 84 years old, died 1 May

1930 in Spartanburg County. The son of Nelson and Lucinda Green, he was buried at Woodruff. Informant—Nelie Green, Woodruff, SC. *(SC Bureau of Vital Statistics, Certificate of Death, 1930 #8911.)*

GREGORY, Coleman
Landrum, Spartanburg County
Cook and servant under Harvey Gregory, 18th Regt, Capt. Robert McBeth
Served 1861–1863
Applied 12 April 1923; approved 24 May 1923
Affidavits: J. W. Gregory and M. H. Randolph
Application #10723: Coleman Gregory, widowed, farmer, 80 years old, died 22 June 1927 in Union County. He was buried at Bethany. Informant—E. D. Gaffney, Jonesville, SC. *(SC Bureau of Vital Statistics, Certificate of Death, 1927 #12280.)*

GRICE, Joe
Dillon, Dillon County
Bodyguard and forager under his master Dr. J. W. Singletary, Co. D, 8th Regt
Served fall 1862–close of war
Applied 4 April 1923; approved 4 April 1923
Affidavits: W. B. Allen and T. C. Sherwood
Application #3216: Joe Grice, widowed, gardener, 96 years old, died 2 February 1934 in Dillon County. The son of Thomas and Scharlott Grice, he was born in Marion, SC. Grice was buried at Hamilton. Informant—J. B. Green, Latta, SC. *(SC Bureau of Vital Statistics, Certificate of Death, 1934 #1981.)*

GRIDISON, William
Arthur's RFD #4, Richland County
Laborer under Capt. Haskell and Capt. Huffman on Sullivan's Island and in Lexington County
Served 1861–1865
Applied 16 April 1923; approved 16 April 1923
Affidavit: Thomas Taylor
Application #9996

GRIFFIN, Ben P.
Pickens, Pickens County
Laborer at Fort Sumter
Served more than one year
Applied 11 April 1923; approved 4 May 1923
Affidavits: J. M. Stewart and James H. Panten. Capt. James A. Griffin, formerly of 4th SC Regiment, said Ben P. Griffin had served.

Application #9667: Ben Griffin, married, about 84 years old, died 22 April 1925 in Pickens County. He was the son of Annie Griffin and was buried in Chicom Cemetery. *(SC Bureau of Vital Statistics, Certificate of Death, 1925 #6550.)*

GUNTER, Harry
604 Gates Street, Columbia, Richland County
Laborer around Charleston, SC
Served for "about eight months"
Applied 19 April 1923; approved 21 April 1923
Affidavit: Francis H. Weston said Gunter was a slave of the deponent's father, Dr. William Weston, and that Gunter "is now and has been for several years, a minister of the gospel" and "a man of unusual intelligence and character."
Application #10003

H

HALTIWANGER, Abe
Newberry RFD #2, Newberry County
Cook under J. O. Turnipseed, Co. E, 3rd Regt, Capt. James D. Nance
Served 1863–April 1865
Applied 18 April 1923; approved 23 April 1923
Affidavit: John W. Gilliam
Application #8507

HAMPTON, Jim
Neals Creek (c/o Jim Elgin, Rt 2, Belton), Anderson County
Servant under Samuel Wilkes, 4th Regt
Served April 1861–July 1862. "Samuel Wilkes was killed in July and I came home with His Body."
Applied 9 April 1923; approved 12 April 1923
Affidavits: A. H. Osborne and J. S. Erskine
Application #850: James Hampton, married, about 90 years old, died 2 July 1925 in Anderson County. He was the son of Ranel Hampton and Emery Webb and was buried at Welfare. Informant—Josephine Hampton, Anderson, SC. *(SC Bureau of Vital Statistics, Certificate of Death, 1925 #11052.)*

HARDY, Derry
Georgetown, Georgetown County
Servant under his master Capt. Calvin Mills (North Carolina)
Entered service in 1861

Applied 15 May 1923
Application #4070: Derry Hardee, widower, laborer, 85 years old, died 21 November 1927 in Georgetown County. He was buried at McDonnel. Informant—W. J. Wilson, undertaker, Georgetown, SC. *(SC Bureau of Vital Statistics, Certificate of Death, 1927 #18390.)*

HARMON, John
Irmo RFD #1, Richland County
Servant under Mid Singley
Served one year
Applied 23 April 1923; approved 1 May 1923
Affidavit: M. S. Meetz
Application #10009: John Harmon, widowed, farmer, 82 years old, died 12 March 1926 in Richland County. He was the son of Adam Harmon and Rosa Miles and was buried at Pine Grove. Informant—Daisy Brannon, Irmo, SC. *(SC Bureau of Vital Statistics, Certificate of Death, 1924 #7361.)*

HARRELL, Scip
Mullins, Marion County
Laborer, Charleston breastworks under E. A. Coleman
Served 1863–1864
Applied 26 May 1923; approved 26 May 1923
Affidavit: J. D. Montgomery
Application # 8015: Sip Harrell, married, 104, died 27 September 1926 in Marion County. He was the son of Dock Kellett and was buried at Old Mill. Informant—Henry Burns, Mullins, SC. *(SC Bureau of Vital Statistics, Certificate of Death, 1926 #20554.)*

HARRIS, Henry
Westminister, Oconee County
Laborer on breastworks under Sam Hester
Served during 1864
Applied 20 April 1923; approved 12 May 1923
Affidavits: H. H. Hester and Georgeana Allen
Application #8980

HARRIS, Joe
Saluda, Saluda County
Servant under John B. Harris, Co. C, 19th Regt, SCV, Capt. John Quattlebaum
Served 28 December 1861–26 April 1865
Applied 19 May 1923; approved 21 May 1923
Affidavits: A. J. Clegg and J. M. Rambo
Application #10371: Joe Harris, married, 95 years old, died 15 April 1931. He worked

as a farm laborer until 1920. He was buried at Pine Hill. Informant—Hubert Harris, Johnston, SC. *(SC Bureau of Vital Statistics, Certificate of Death, 1931 #9562.)*

HARRISON, Alex
Aiken, Aiken County
Servant under Col. Olin Dantzen, Co. B, 20th Regt, Capt. P. A. McMichael
Served 1 January 1861–31 December 1863
Applied 3 March 1924; approved 23 April 1924
Affidavits: Simon Pinckney and D. W. Seigler
Application #354

HARRISON, Gus
Aiken, Aiken County
Servant under Guss White
Served 1862–1865
Applied 8 May 1923; approved 8 May 1923
Affidavits: Joe Brunson and J. A. M. Gardner
Application #355

HARRISON, March, Sr
Aiken, Aiken County
Servant under James Foster and Haus Boatwright, Co. B, 14th Regt, Capt. Tillman Watson
Served early 1861–end of war 1865
Applied 20 April 1923; approved 8 May 1923
Affidavits: R. B. Watson and C. B. Crouch
Application #356

HARRISON, Warren
Ninety-Six, Greenwood County
Servant under Gen. Mort Gary, Capt. Summerfield Gary
Served 1864–1865
Applied 14 April 1923
Affidavit: H. P. Galphin
Application #5920

HART, Tillman
Johnston, Edgefield County
Cook under John W. Bartley, Co. K, 7th Regt, Capt. Bradley
Served 1861–9 April 1865
Applied 28 April 1923; approved 4 May 1923
Affidavits: J. Russell Wright and B. Wallace Wright
Application #3545

HAY, Cato
Barnwell, Barnwell County
Laborer building batteries under Easterling and Weathersbee. Easterling was overseer.
Served two months
Applied 12 April 1923; approved 16 April 1923
Affidavits: J. Ancel Meyer and J. Staff Halford
Application #1403

HAYNES, Jenkins
Brunson RFD, Hampton County
Cook under Claudius Haynes, Co. A, 3rd SC Cav, Capt. Lowery
Served 1862–surrender 1865
Applied 14 May 1923; approved 14 May 1923
Application #6136

HEARST, Wesley
Greenwood, Greenwood County
Cook under Capt. Tim (or Tom) Lipscomb, Co. A
Served April 1862–April 1865
Applied 14 April 1923
Affidavit: Josephene Hearst
Application #5924

HENRY, Addison
Laurens No. 4, Laurens County
Cook and attendant under Sudy Teague, John Finley, and William Finley, Co. A, 3rd Btn, SC Inf, Capt. Townsend
Served April 1861–May 1862
Applied 20 April 1923; approved 21 April 1923
Affidavits: J. W. Henry and H. A. Martin
Application #7135

HIERS, Lawton
Bamberg, Bamberg County
Laborer under Capt. J. S. Bamberg, Co. C, 1st Regt
Served 1861–1862
Applied 8 May 1923; approved 8 May 1923
Affidavits: J. C. Copeland and J. I. Copeland
Application #1214

HILL, Adam
Ridge Spring, Saluda County

Cook under John Kellar, Co. C, 6th Cav, Capt. Peter W. Goodwin
Served spring 1863–9 April 1865
Applied 20 April 1923; approved 21 May 1923
Affidavits: R. B. Watson and C. B. Crouch.
Application #10375

HINTON, Joseph
Eastover, Richland County
Servant under William F. Seay, Co. M, 7th Regt, Capt. Brooks
Served 1862–1865
Applied 24 April 1923; approved 27 April 1923
Affidavit: T. N. Seay
Application #10029

HOBSON, Sylvester
Spartanburg, Spartanburg County
Servant under Capt. William S. Hobson, Co. B, 4th Regt, SC State Troops
Served August 1864–April 1865
Applied 16 April 1923; approved 24 May 1923
Affidavits: W. E. Thomson and J. M. Greer. On 11 April 1923 in Aberdeen, Mississippi, William S. Hobson said Silvester Hobson had served with him as a servant and cook.
Application #10771

HODGES, George
Cokesbury, Greenwood County
Cook under Capt. Higgins, Orr's Regt
Served 1862–1865
Applied 19 May 1923; approved 20 May 1923
Affidavit: M. J. Higgins
Application #5929

HOLMES, Gilbert
Orangeburg, Orangeburg County
Servant under Eddie Andrews
Served more than six months
Applied 11 April 1923; approved 16 May 1924
Affidavits: J. D. Oliver and Shepherd Banks
Application #9336

HOOD, Thomas
Laurens, Laurens County
Laborer, fortifications, Charleston and islands

Served more than six months
Applied 19 April 1923; approved 15 May 1923
Affidavits: W. S. Culbertson and H. H. Blackwell
Application #7143

HOOK, William (known during the Civil War as William Dannelly)
North, Orangeburg County
Servant under Dr. Dick Dannelly. Hook also "thre[w] up brea[s]tworks on James Island under command of Capt Gregg—and on Sullivans Island—also worked on brea[s]tworks at Hamptons race track near Columbia."
Served 1861–1865
Applied 22 May 1923; approved 26 May 1923
Affidavits: Nancy A. McMichael and J. S. Craft. Mrs. Martha North, "now too feeble to sign," confirmed that Hook was the "servant of Dr. Dick Dannelly."
Application #9338

HOWARD, Steven
Ninety-Six, Greenwood County
Laborer and cook under Capt. Williams
Served spring 1862–close of war 1865
Applied 28 April 1923; approved 7 May 1923
Affidavits: Charles E. Sullivan and H. D. Rogers
Application #5932

HOWELL, Emanuel
St. Matthews, Calhoun County
Servant under Townsend
Served about a year
Applied 7 May 1923; approved 7 May 1923
Affidavits: H. D. Paulling and Mrs. W. C. Paulling
Application #1698

HUNTER, Tom
Ora, Laurens County
Cook and attendant under Dr. J. P. Hunter, Co. G, 3rd Regt, SC Inf, Capt. R. P. Todd
Served 15 April 1861–October 1863
Applied 10 April 1923; approved 19 April 1923
Affidavits: Mel Fleming and T. Y. Henderson
Application #7149

HUTCHERSON, Charles
Greenwood RFD #6, Greenwood County
Cook under Sole Hutcherson, Co. F, 2nd Regt, Capt. W. C. Vance

African Americans labor on Confederate fortifications, James Island, S.C. Joseph T. Wilson, ***Black Phalanx*** *(N.Y.:De Capo Press, 1994). Reprint of the 1887 ed.*

Served 1861–1865
Applied 7 May 1923; approved 7 May 1923
Affidavit: A. B. Ellis
Application #5934

J

***JACKSON, Griffin**
Hodges, Greenwood County
Cook under John Clavert, 2nd SC Rifles
Served 1864–April 1865
Applied 12 April 1923
Affidavits: T. C. Seal and D. T. Hannah
Application: #5936

JACOBS, Richard
Barnwell, Barnwell County
Laborer "under government control"
Served 1863–1864

Applied 28 April 1923; approved 28 April 1923
Affidavits: J. Staff Halford and L. F. Hair
Application #1409

JAGGERS, Charles
Columbia, Richland County
Teamster under Capt. Boyd, Co. H, Rions Btn
Served April 1862–9 April 1865
Applied 4 April 1923; approved 11 April 1923
Affidavits: J. E. Weir and W. B. P. Weir said he served under L. A. Easters
Application #10054

JAMES, Charles
259 W. Henry, Spartanburg, Spartanburg County
Cook under William T. Chappell, Gunells Btn
Served 1861–1862
Applied 25 April 1924; approved 14 June 1924
Affidavits: Mary E. Hudgens and Sarah Tranks
Application #10793

JAMISON, Aaron
Allendale, Allendale County
Cook under Capt. Estes, Co. K, 3rd Regt, SC Cav, Capt. W. B. Peeples
Served 1861–1865
Applied 10 May 1923; approved 28 May 1923
Affidavits: John Logan and J. W. Thomas
Application #589

JENKINS, Esaw
Harleyville, Dorchester County
Cook under John Nettles, Co. D, 2nd Regt, Capt. Hydrick
Served January 1861–1865
Applied 9 April 1923
Affidavit: Jacob Lee
Application #3372

***JENKINS, Jeff**
Spartanburg, Spartanburg County
Servant under Dr. Thomas Zimmerman, Capt. Elson Keitt
Served 1863–1865
Applied 30 Jan. 1924; approved 14 June 1924
Affidavits: Elias Evans and Adam Evans
Application #10797

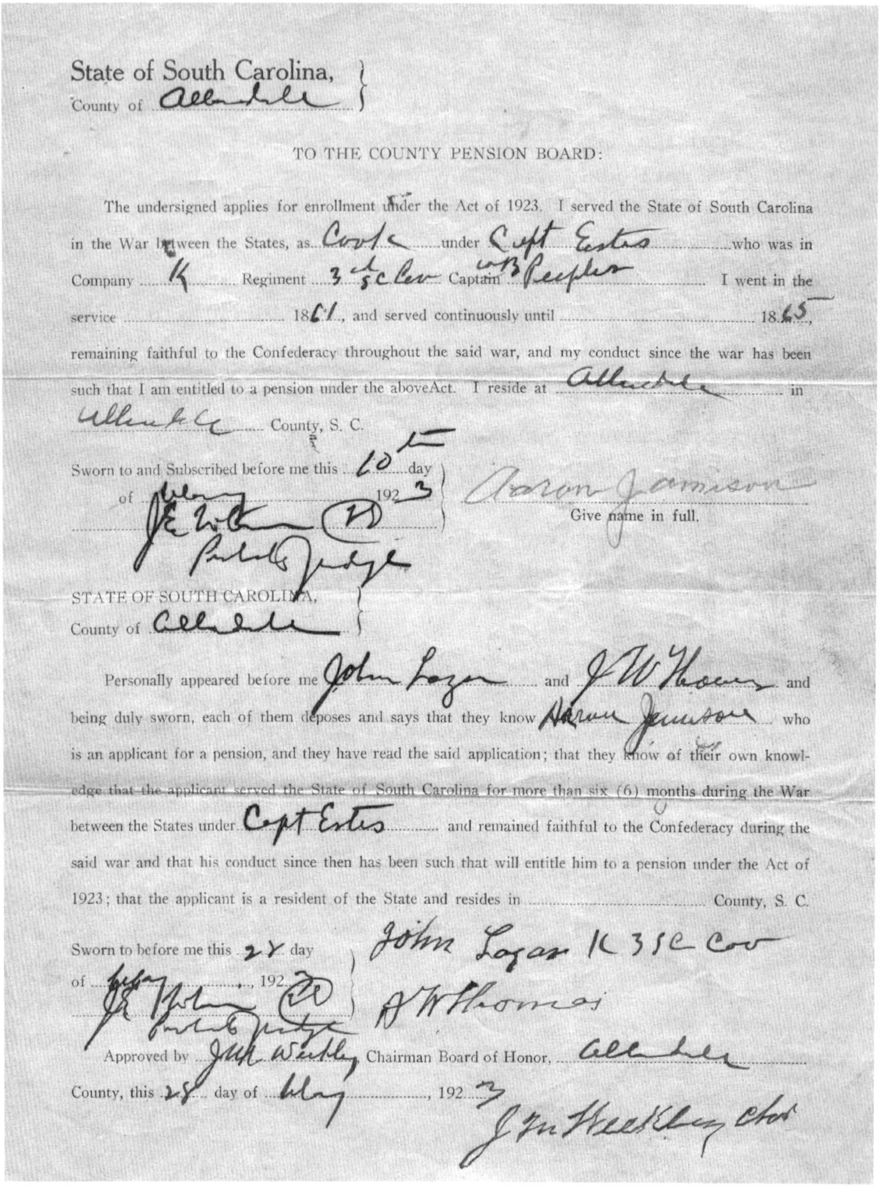

State of South Carolina,
County of Allendale

TO THE COUNTY PENSION BOARD:

The undersigned applies for enrollment under the Act of 1923. I served the State of South Carolina in the War between the States, as Cook under Capt Estes who was in Company K Regiment 3rd S C Cav Captain W B Peeples I went in the service 1861, and served continuously until 1865, remaining faithful to the Confederacy throughout the said war, and my conduct since the war has been such that I am entitled to a pension under the aboveAct. I reside at Allendale in Allendale County, S. C.

Sworn to and Subscribed before me this 10th day of May 1923
J E Wilson (?) Probate Judge

Aaron Jamison
Give name in full.

STATE OF SOUTH CAROLINA,
County of Allendale

Personally appeared before me John Logan and J W Thomas and being duly sworn, each of them deposes and says that they know Aaron Jamison who is an applicant for a pension, and they have read the said application; that they know of their own knowledge that the applicant served the State of South Carolina for more than six (6) months during the War between the States under Capt Estes and remained faithful to the Confederacy during the said war and that his conduct since then has been such that will entitle him to a pension under the Act of 1923; that the applicant is a resident of the State and resides in .... County, S. C.

Sworn to before me this 28 day of May, 1923
J E Wilson (?) Probate Judge

John Logan K 3 SC Cav
J W Thomas

Approved by J W Weekley Chairman Board of Honor, Allendale County, this 28 day of May, 1923
J W Weekley Chm

Pension application for Aaron Jamison. Records of the Comptroller General, Pension Applications, 1919–1926, #589. SCDAH.

JENKINS, Jethro
Mt. Pleasant, Charleston County
Servant under Capt. Cornelius Sams, Capt Elias Venning
Served 1863–1865

Applied 27 September 1923; approved 4 April 1924
Affidavits: Mrs. J. Rutledge Smith and Mrs. Nancy Scott
Application #1843

JOHNSON, Edward
St. Matthews, Calhoun County
Cook and helper under Tolin Bass, Co. H, 2nd Regt, Capt. McFane
Served July 1862–February 1865
Applied 4 May 1923
Affidavits: H. C. Paulling and J. D. Antley
Application #1699

JOHNSON, Hector
Ridgeville, Dorchester County
Served with Co. D, 11th Regt
Served until end of war
Applied 18 May 1923; approved 24 May 1924
Affidavits: Jerry Elias Hinton and T. F. Mizell
Application #3371: Hector Johnson, widowed, farmer, 106 years old, died 20 November 1931 in Dorchester County. He was born 25 December 1825. His wife was Carrie White. He was the son of Ben Johnson and Celia Greenhorn. Informant—Ralph Johnson, Ridgeville, SC. *(SC Bureau of Vital Statistics, Certificate of Death, 1931 #17834.)*

JOHNSON, Henry
McClellanville (P. O. Cross), Berkeley County
Laborer under Pvt. Oliver Russell, Co. H, 11th Regt, Capt. Christopher Gaillard
Served 1861–1865
Applied 25 January 1927
Affidavits; Louisa Nash and Alice Jennett
Application #1612

***JOHNSON, Merriman**
St. Paul, Clarendon County
Servant under Ellison A. Smyth, Co. B, 44th Regt, Capt. D. J. Bradham
Served November 1864–surrender
Applied 16 April 1923; approved 27 April 1923
Affidavit: Ellison H. Smyth
Application #2767

JOHNSON, Noh
Columbia, Richland County
Servant under Capt. McFie, Co. C, 2nd Regt

Served 1861–11 April 1865
Applied 11 April 1923; approved 11 April 1923
Affidavit: W. S. Green
Application #10057: Noah Johnson, a widowed carpenter, 97 years old, died 27 May 1930 in Richland County. He was the son of Martha Johnson and was buried in Randolph Cemetery. Informant—Dr. F. B. Johnson. *(SC Bureau of Vital Statistics, Certificate of Death, 1930 #8685.)*

***JOHNSON, Preston**
Marion RFD #1, Marion County
Laborer, fortifications at Charleston
Approved 26 May 1923 by Marion County Board of Honor
Application #8104

JOHNSON, Robert
c/o W. F. Ewart, Newberry, Newberry County
Cook under Dr. David E. Ewart, Co. E, 3rd Regt, Capt. James D. Nance
Served 1861–1864
Applied 7 April 1923; approved 23 April 1923
Affidavits: William Y. Fair and R. T. Caldwell
Application #8541

JONES, Henry
Lowndesville, Abbeville County
Cook under Capt. White
Served 1863–1865
Applied 25 April 1923; approved 28 April 1923
Affidavit: W. T. Cunningham
Application #100: Henry Jones, married, 87 years old, died 18 March 1933 in Abbeville County. He was the son of Dan Jones and was buried in Smyrna. Informant—John W. Jones, Lowndesville, SC. *(SC Bureau of Vital Statistics, Certificate of Death, 1933 #7684.)*

JONES, William
Orangeburg, Orangeburg County
Cook under Benjamin Izlar, Capt. Alfred Frederick
Served until "close of war" 1865
Applied 6 April 1923; approved 24 April 1923
Affidavit: G. L. Salley
Application #9375: William Jones, a married farmer, 110 years old, died 31 August 1934 in Orangeburg County. The son of Nancy and Frank Jones, he was buried in Jerusalem Cemetery. Informant—Susan Jones, Orangeburg, SC. *(SC Bureau of Vital Statistics, Certificate of Death, 1934 #13128.)*

K

KEARSE, Preston
Olar, Bamberg County
Servant under Tom Ealy, worked on fortifications
Served June 1864–February 1865
Applied 26 May 1923; approved 26 May 1923
Affidavits: J. B. Kearse and J. J. Kearse
Application #1230

KEEL, Daniel
Barnwell, Barnwell County
Cook under Mike O'Dowd, 2nd SC Art, Capt. Lagree
Served June 1862–April 1865
Applied 9 April 1923; approved 9 April 1923
Affidavits: J. Ansel Meyer and J. Staff Halford
Application #1420

KELLY, Ansel
Jackson, Aiken County
Cook under G. W. Stallings, Co. G, 2nd Regt, SC Art
Served 1861–1865
Applied 23 April 1923
Affidavits: J. A. Meyer and J. Staff Halford
Application #396

KNIGHT, L. K.
West Union, Oconee County
Cook under Dr. J. P. Knight, Co. A, Hamptons Brigade. Knight said he was wounded near Richmond in 1864.
Served 1861–1865
Applied 20 April 1923; approved 20 April 1923
Affidavits: Sarah Ida Knight said L. K. Knight was a "family" servant and served during the Civil War with her father, Dr. James Perry Knight of Laurens County. She also said L. K. Knight was wounded "around Petersburg" and is "now blind at 86 years of age."
Application #9009: Louis Knight, a widowed farmer, 94 years old, died 9 August 1925 in Oconee County. He was born in Laurens County and buried in Pleasant Grove Churchyard. Informant—Sam Knight, West Union, SC. (*SC Bureau of Vital Statistics, Certificate of Death, 1925 #14211.*)

*Francis T. Miller, ed., **The Photographic History of the Civil War,** vol. 9 (N.Y.: The Review of Reviews Co., 1911).*

L

LADSON, S. W.
Adams Run, Charleston County
Cook in Washington's Art, Capt. George H. Walter
Served 1863–1865
Applied 18 March 1924; approved 24 March 1924
Affidavit: William Culbert
Application #1849

LARK, Summerfield
Newberry, Newberry County
Cook under Dennis Lark, 3rd SC Cav, Capt. Gary
Served 1861–April 1865
Applied 4 April 1923; approved 23 April 1923
Affidavits: William Y. Fair and R. T. Caldwell
Application #8559: Sumer L. Lark, a married farmer, born 1821, died 3 November 1925 in Newberry County. He was the son of Andrew and Mary Lark and was 104 years old when he died. Lark was buried in Werts Cemetery. Informant—Andrew Lark, Newberry, SC. *(SC Bureau of Vital Statistics, Certificate of Death, 1925 #19292.)*

LAURELL, Bill
Pineland, Jasper County
Cook under J. E. Robinson, Co. C, 3rd Regt, Capt. Gregory

Served 1864–1865
Applied 2 February 1925; approved 5 February 1925
Affidavits: G. W. Tuten and Benj. F. Langford
Application #6504

LAWRENCE, Esau
Santee, Georgetown County
Hostler under Cpl. G. G. Ford, Capt. John Tucker
Served 1861–1865
Applied 28 April 1923; approved 23 May 1923
Affidavit: W. B. Thompson
Application #4077

***LAWTON, Charles**
Orangeburg, Orangeburg County
Cook under William Townsend, father of Judge Townsend, Beaufort Light Artillery, Capt. Stephen Elliott
Served 1861–1865
Applied 3 April 1923; approved 18 April 1923
Affidavit: W. H. Townsend said Lawton served with his father, William Hutson Townsend from McPhersonville, with the Beaufort Light Artillery, first under Capt. Stephen Elliott and then under Capt. H. M. Stuart. Townsend also said Lawton relocated to Orangeburg on the advice of Townsend's grand uncle, William Maine Hutson, an attorney there. W. H. Townsend was a circuit judge who lived in Columbia.
Application #9389: Charlie Lawton, married, 86 years old, died 17 June 1928 in Orangeburg County. Lawton was born in Beaufort County and was a carpenter. His parents were Betsey Lloyd and Charlie Lawton, Sr. Lawton was buried in Orangeburg, SC. Informant—Saul Lawton, Orangeburg, SC. *(SC Bureau of Vital Statistics, Certificate of Death, 1928 #11028.)*

LEE, Jacob
Jedburg, Dorchester County
Attendant, John Henry Browning, Stephen Browning, and J. Browning, Co. D, 2nd SC Cav, Capt. Hydrick
Served until end of war
Applied 7 April 1923; approved 30 April 1923
Affidavit: T. C. Harvey
Application #3380: Jacob Lee, widowed and probably between 70 and 80 years old, died 27 March 1929 in Dorchester County. He was the son of Ned Lee and was buried at St. Johns Church, Berkeley County. Informant—Simon Lee, Jedburg, SC. *(SC Bureau of Vital Statistics, Certificate of Death, 1929 #4451.)*

LEMON, Willis
Reevesville, Dorchester County
Servant under Dr. Aquilla Johnston, Capt. Isaac Johnston
Served January 1862–April 1865
Applied 9 April 1923; approved 30 April 1923
Affidavits: J. H. Carr and Pompey Rivers
Application #3382

LEWIS, W. S.
37 Kennedy Street, Charleston, Charleston County
Servant under James Thurston, Marine Corps, CSS *Atalanta,* and later with Edward N. Thurston until end of war
Applied 9 April 1923; approved 14 April 1923
Affidavit: Robert T. Ravenel
Application #1854
William S. Lewis, a married brick mason, 89 years old, died 8 February 1929 in Charleston County. He was the son of Adele and William Lewis and was buried at Zion Presbyterian Church. Informant—Mrs. Wainwright, 37 Kennedy Street, Charleston, SC. *(SC Bureau of Vital Statistics, Certificate of Death, 1929 #2453.)*

LIGHTNER (Leitner), Alex
Avon (PO Shelton), Fairfield County
Cook under Butler Estes, 3rd Btn, Capt. John McLurkin, Major Giles
Served April 1863–9 April 1865
Applied 16 February 1924; approved 22 April 1924
Affidavits: T. L. Estes and A. Dunbar
Application #3736

LLOYD, Chance
Blackville, Barnwell County
Cook under Maj. W. W. Hutto, Co. C, 8th Btn, Capt. C. C. Cooper
Served April 1864–April 1865
Applied 28 April 1923; approved 4 May 1923
Affidavits: F. N. Hair and L. F. Cave
Application #1426

LOADHOLT, Miles
Jennys, Allendale County
Cook under D. O. Loadholt and A. R. Loadholt, 3rd Regt, Smart's Co
Served 1862–close of war, 1865
Applied 2 October 1923
Affidavits: H. W. Dees and J. D. Jenny
Application #601: Miles Loadholt, widowed, 85 years old, died 6 January 1929 in

Allendale County. The son of a Stokes and Liel Loadholt, he adopted his mother's surname. Loadholt was born in Barnwell County and buried at Cherry Grove. Informant—Willie Loadholt, Fairfax, SC. *(SC Bureau of Vital Statistics, Certificate of Death, 1929 #2231.)*

LOGAN, West
Ninety-Six, Greenwood County
Cook and laundryman under Jim, Bill and Pinckney Morrow and Ed Smith, Co. F, 2nd SCV, Capt. Bill Perriman
Served thirty months, beginning 1862
Applied 5 May 1923; approved 10 May 1923
Affidavits: B. L. Kinard and A. B. Ellis
Application #8925: West Logan, widowed, farmer, 100 years 11 months old, died 10 March 1927 in Greenwood County. The son of Aggie Lewis and Merlfis Logan, he was born in Abbeville and buried at Enore Zion. Informant—J. R. Dean, undertaker, Ninety Six, SC. *(SC Bureau of Vital Statistics, Certificate of Death, 1927 #3920.)*

***LOGAN, William B.**
Servant under R. D. Zimmerman, 25 Regt SCV, Capt. Sellers
Served "nearly the whole war"
Source: List submitted by Thomas E. Richardson, judge of probate, Sumter County, 13 June 1923. Richardson also said Logan was originally from Orangeburg and served in a hospital after his master was killed at Petersburg.
Application #11276b: William B. Logan, a married farmer, 82 years 2 months 15 days old, died 25 December 1925 in Sumter County. He was born 10 October 1943 in Spartanburg County and buried in the Walker Cemetery. Informant—Willie H. Jones, Sumter, SC. *(SC Bureau of Vital Statistics, Certificate of Death, 1925 #21830.)*

LONG, Daniel Albright
Florence, Florence County
Service under Col. Wash, Co. C, 2nd Regt, NC
Served 1862–25 April 1865
Applied 1 April 1927; approved 2 May 1927
Affidavits not present
Application #3947

M

MACK, Sam
279 Ashley Avenue, Charleston, Charleston County
Cook under Capt. Julius Shanklin, 4th SC Regt
Served 1861

Applied 24 April 1923; approved 24 April 1923
Affidavit: I. W. Hirsch and Earle Sloan. Sloan said that to his knowledge, Hirsch was "the only surviving member" of his father's "old regiment living in Charleston" and that he understood Sam Mack "was one of the slaves of the Shanklins (of Pendleton, SC) and that he accompanied Capt. Julian Shanklin as body servant."
Application #1862

MAKIN, Matthew
Cokesbury, Greenwood County
Servant under A. W. Moore, Col. Butler's Regt
Served until April 1865
Applied 14 April 1923
Affidavit: E. C. Connor
Application #5957

MATTISON, Marshall
Belton RFD #1, Anderson County
Cook under Wyatt Mattison, Provost Guard, Columbia, SC, Capt. R. D. Senn
Served March or April 1864–December 1864
Applied 16 April 1923; approved 30 April 1923
Affidavits: J. A. Brock and L. E. Campbell
Application #939: Marshall Mattison, married, farmer, 77 years old, died 25 August 1927 in Anderson County. He was the son of Docie and Nelson Mattison and was born 2 April 1850. He was buried at Mt. Zion. Informant—Josephine Clinkscale, Rt. 3, Belton, SC. *(SC Bureau of Vital Statistics, Certificate of Death, 1927 #142888.)*

MCALLISTER, Andrew
Abbeville, Abbeville County
Cook, Co. G, 1st Regt, Capt. J. L. Johnson
Served 1862–close of war 1865
Applied 24 May 1924; approved 26 May 1924
Affidavits: J. S. Williams and J. H. Penney
Application #128

MCCANT, Alex
Pinopolis, Berkeley County
Servant under Charles S. Edwards, Co. A, 5th Regt, Capt. John C. Edward
Served c.1861–close of war 1865
Applied 30 April 1923; approved 30 April 1923
Affidavits: J. A. Harvey and J. W. McCants
Application #1619: Alex McCant, widowed, farmer, 89 years old, died 20 October

1923 in Berkeley County. He was the son of Alex McCant and was born 1 September 1839 in Dorchester County. He was buried in St. James Cemetery. Informant—Alex McCants, Jr., Pinopolis, SC. *(SC Bureau of Vital Statistics, Certificate of Death, 1923 #15419.)*

MCCLINTOCK, Perry
Clinton, Laurens County
Laborer (slave of Robert McClintock of Laurens County) on James Island Fortifications
Served ten months in 1863
Applied 9 April 1923; approved 14 May 1923
Affidavits: J. H. M. Young and R. P. Adair, Sr.
Application #7192: Perry McClintock, widowed, farmer 95 years old, died 4 May 1929 in Laurens County. He was buried at New Grove. Informant—Bill McClintock, Laurens, SC. *(SC Bureau of Vital Statistics, Certificate of Death, 1929 #8609.)*

MCCLINTON, Jack
Due West, Abbeville County
Cook under Capt. T. S. Ellis, Co. G, Orr's Regt
Served 1864–1865
Applied 28 May 1923; approved 28 May 1923
Application #130: Jack McClinton, married, retired farmer, 94 years old, died 4 September 1930. His wife was Ella McClinton. He was born in Virginia and buried at Due West. Informant—Ella McClinton, Due West, SC. *(SC Bureau of Vital Statistics, Certificate of Death, 1930 #14906.)*

MCDONALD, Bob
State Park, Richland County
Servant
Served 1861–1865
Applied 13 April 1923; approved 14 April 1923
Affidavit: John Thomas
Application #10120

MCDONALD, Bristow
Elliott, Lee County
Servant under William Luckey, Co. E, 19th Regt, Capt. Clinkscales
Applied 23 April 1923; approved 24 May 1923
Affidavits: H. W. Scott and Judge D. Newman
Application #7488: Bristow McDonald, widowed, farmer, about 90 years old, died 30 June 1931 in Lee County. His wife was Laura McDonald. He was the son of Susan Davis. He was born at Wysackey and was buried there. Informant—

McDonald, Wysackey, SC. *(SC Bureau of Vital Statistics, Certificate of Death, 1931 #13636.)*

MCDONALD, Mitchell
Elliotts, Lee County
Laborer under Capt. Anderson
Served 1862–1863
Applied 23 May 1923; approved 24 May 1923
Affidavit: Alvin Solomon
***Application #7487*:** This might be Michel McDonald, married, farmer, 81 years old, who died 20 February 1924 in Lee County. McDonald was the son of Harriet DuRant and Jake McDonald and was born in Sumter County. Informant—Oliver Soloman, Elliott, SC. *(SC Bureau of Vital Statistics, Certificate of Death, 1924 #2814.)*

MCELRATH, Tom
Woodruff, Spartanburg County
Servant under Capt. G. B. Dean, 2nd Cav Regt
Served 1862–April 1865
Applied 23 April 1923; approved 24 May 1923
Affidavits: J. W. Westmoreland and A. D. Chamblin
Application #10887

MCFADDEN, Rufus
Harleyville, Dorchester County
Cook under Capt. Thomas Fraser, Lancaster Graves Regt, Capt. Landing
Served 1861–end of war 1861
Applied 5 May 1923; approved 26 May 1924
Affidavit: Dr. A. M. Fraser
***Application #3386*:** Rufas McFadden, a widowed farmer, 98 years, 1 month and 1 day old, died 4 March 1932 in Dorchester County. His wife was Julia Addison. He was the son of Lavina Bennett and S. McFadden and was born 10 February 1932 [sic] in North Carolina. McFadden was buried in Dorchester Cemetery. Informant—Bill McFadden, Harleyville, SC. *(SC Bureau of Vital Statistics, Certificate of Death, 1932 # 3501.)*

MCKINLEY, John
Charleston, Charleston County
Served as private, Charleston Riflemen, 14th Regt, Capt. Joe Johnson
Served January 1861–April 9, 1866
Applied 22 March 1928; approved 26 March 1928
Affidavits: S. E. Welch and W. R. Greer
Application #1872

MCLEOD, John
North, Orangeburg County
Servant under Dr. B. H. Knotts, Co. K, 2nd Regt Cav, Capt. Williams
Served October 1863–September 1865
Applied 9 April 1923; approved 18 April 1923
Affidavit: Dr. B. H. Knotts
Application #9400

MCNEILL, Hector
Dillon, Dillon County
Waitman under James Manning, Co. I, 20th Regt, Capt. A. D. Sparks
Served spring 1864–spring 1865
Applied 11 April 1923; approved 12 May 1923
Affidavits: D. McLaurin and T. C. Sherwood
Application #3258

MCTEER, Caesar (Cezar)
Hampton, Hampton County
Cook under Edwin McTeer, Co. A, 3rd SC Cav, Capt. Lowery
Served 1862–end of war 1865
Applied 14 May 1923; approved 14 May 1923
***Application #6150*:** Caezar McTeer, widower, about 80 years old, died 7 October 1931 in Hampton County. He was buried in Rivers Graveyard. Informant—Porter Weyman, Early Branch, SC. *(SC Bureau of Vital Statistics, Certificate of Death, 1931 #16614.)*

MIDDLETON, Louis
18 Montague Street, Charleston County
Cook under R. B. Simons, Co. A, SC Siege Train, Capt. B. C. Webb
Applied 24 April 1923; approved April 1923
Affidavits: R. B. Simons and T. Grange Simons
Application #1981

MIKELL, Wallace
18 Pine Street, Charleston, Charleston County
Camp attendant under Sidney Legare, Signal Corps, Capt. Micah Jenkins
Served 1861–1865
Applied 8 January 1923; approved 4 April 1924
Affidavit: Eliza H. Glover, with annotation "For further reference see E. T. Legare, St. Andrews Parish, S. C."
Application #1879

MILANS, Nelson
Mountville, Laurens County

Confederate camp on Stono Inlet near Charleston, S.C. Library of Congress.

Laborer, Sea Island fortifications
Served more than six months
Applied 30 April 1923; approved 1 May 1923
Affidavits: B. Goodman and W. B. Fuller
Application #7203: Nelson Milan, married, farmer, about 95 years old, died 27 February 1924 in Laurens County. He was the son of Millie Carter and Reuben Ligon and was buried at New Hope. Informant—Joe Milan, Mountville, SC. *(SC Bureau of Vital Statistics, Certificate of Death, 1924 #8794.)*

MILEY, James
Aiken, Aiken County
Servant under his owner, John Wiley, Colcock's Regt, SCV, Capt. Henry Smart
Served 1861–summer 1864
Applied 30 May 1923; approved 2 June 1923
Affidavits: H. H. Wyman, Sr., MD, and J. Frampton Wyman, MD
Application #421: James Miley, married, laborer, 80 years old, died 16 May 1925 in Aiken County. The son of Mary, he was buried in the African American cemetery in Aiken. Informant—Mrs. James Miley, Aiken, SC. *(SC Bureau of Vital Statistics, Certificate of Death, 1925 #7036.)*

MILLER, Berry
Latta, Dillon County
Servant under his owner, Capt. Miller, Co. B, 10th Regt, SCV
Served August 1861–August 1862
Applied 26 May 1923
Affidavit: Trus Franklin and L. T. Sessions
Application #8044: Berry Miller, married, farmer, 80 years old, died 22 July 1924 in Dillon County. Born in North Carolina. He was buried at Fork Chapel. Informant—Lanier Miller, Latta, SC. *(SC Bureau of Vital Statistics, Certificate of Death, 1924 #14529.)*

MILLER, Kelly
Winnsboro, Fairfield County
Servant under Capt. John Bell, Co. F, 12th Regt, SC Inf, Capt. H. McMakin
Served April 1862–surrender 1865
Applied 21 April 1923; approved 28 April 1923
Application #3757

MIMS, Dallas
McCormick Rt 3, McCormick County
Servant under Luke Shibley, Co. K, 7th Regt, Capt. Jack Burriss
Served 1861 for a year or two until he brought his master home in ill health. Shibley died.
Applied 23 April 1923; approved 28 April 1923
Affidavits: J. M. Mims and W. E. Sheppard
Application #8190: Dallas Mims, married, farmer, 106 years old, died 27 February 1930 in McCormick County. He was the son of Samuel Mims and was buried at Bailey Bethel Church. Informant—S. B. Mims, McCormick, SC. *(SC Bureau of Vital Statistics, Certificate of Death, 1930 #2695.)*

MITCHELL, Rev. June
Orangeburg, Orangeburg County
Servant under his owner, Dr. Albert Tabor, Fort Motte Rangers, Capt. Trezevant

Served 1861–close of war 1865
Applied 7 April 1923; approved 18 April 1923
Affidavits: Mrs. Albert R. Taber, Sr., (widow of Dr. Albert Tabor) and William C. Wolfe
***Application #9408*:** June Mitchel, married, bricklayer, 87 years old, died 22 May 1931 in Orangeburg County. He was the son of Lewis Mitchell and was buried in Orangeburg. Informant—Addison Wright, Orangeburg, SC. *(SC Bureau of Vital Statistics, Certificate of Death, 1931 #8384.)*

***MITCHELL, Theodore**
Pomaria, Newberry County
Cook under Riley Boys, Co. B, Orrs Rifles, SCV, Capt. Perrin
Served 1861–1863
Applied 17 April 1923; approved 8 May 1923
Application #8600

MOBLEY, Harrison
Winnsboro, Fairfield County
CSA Army
Served six months
Applied 30 April 1923; approved 30 April 1923
Application #3758

MOBLEY, Richmond
Saluda, Saluda County
Cook and laundryman under Billie Mobley, Co. E, 1st Regt, SC State Troops, Capt. John Mickler
Served November 1864–April 1865
Applied 15 April 1923; approved 21 May 1923
Affidavits: W. F. Mobley and J. G. Mobley
***Application #10414*:** Richman Mabby, unmarried, farmer 87 years old, died 6 March 1932 in Saluda County. Place of burial indecipherable. Informant—Sunar Ellins. *(SC Bureau of Vital Statistics, Certificate of Death, 1932 #4317.)*

MOORE, Hiram
Winnsboro, Fairfield County
Cook under Capt. Mike Moore
Served 1862–1865
Applied 11 May 1924; approved 11 May 1924
***Application #3759*:** Hiram Moore, widowed, laborer, 86 years old, died 25 August 1928 in Richland County. He was born in Chester in 1842 and was the son of Abram Moore. He was buried at Crane Creek. Informant—James Moore, Richland County. *(SC Bureau of Vital Statistics, Certificate of Death, 1928 #15222.)*

MORGAN, Alford
Newberry, Newberry County
Cook under three Beam Boys, CSA
Served 1861–April 1865
Applied 6 April 1923; approved 23 April 1923
Affidavits: J. H. Alewine and E. S. Cromer
Application #8607: Alford Morgan, married, day laborer, 75 years old, died 22 May 1923 in Newberry County. He was born in 1848 and was the son of Salley and Manas Morgan. He was buried at Enoree Church. Informant—John Wilson, Newberry, SC. *(SC Bureau of Vital Statistics, Certificate of Death, 1923 #8181.)*

MOULTRIE, Sheddrick
Georgetown, Georgetown County
Orderly under Capt. James Trapier
Served 1861–1865
Applied 9 May 1923
Affidavits: J. R. May and F. L. Sian
Application #4086

MURPHY, Robert
Longtown, Kershaw County
Cook under Joe Huckabee, Co. D, 15th SCV, Capt. Tom Warren
Served 1861–1865
Applied 3 April 1923; approved 16 April 1923
Affidavits: W. J. Spradley and Henry Truesdel
Application #6660: Robert Murphy, widowed, farmer, 89 years old, died 5 July 1924 in Kershaw County. He was the son of Eliza and Joe Murphy and was buried at Mt. Joshua. Informant—June Murphy, Camden, SC. *(SC Bureau of Vital Statistics, Certificate of Death, 1924 #13105.)*

MYERS, Robert
St. Charles, Lee County
Servant under Capt. Spratts, Co. I, 49th Regt, Capt. Mills
Served September 1863–1864
Applied 5 May 1923; approved 24 May 1923
Affidavits: H. W. Scott and J. T. Clark
Application #7495

N

NIMMONS, Will
Barnwell, Barnwell County

Laborer, James Island, 2nd Art
Applied 9 April 1923; approved 9 April 1923
Affidavits: J. Ansel Meyer and J. Staff Halford
Application #1451: Will Nimmons, single, farm worker, 89 years old, died 12 May 1924 in Barnwell County. He was the son of Seullie Odom and Albert Nimmons and was buried in Barnwell. Informant—Howard Nimmons, Barnwell, SC. *(SC Bureau of VItal Statistics, Certificate of Death, 1924 #9984.)*

O

OWENS, Starling
Pendleton RFD #1, Anderson County
Cook under B. L. Thompson, 4th Regt, SC Cav, Capt. Rivers
Served 1862–close of war 1865
Applied 20 April 1923; approved 11 May 1923
Affidavits: L. R. Thompson and J. T. McAbee
Application #1002: Starling Owens, married, farmer, 100 years old, died 23 March 1930 in Anderson County. He was the son of Annie and George Owens and was buried at Mt. Pisgah. Informant—Amanda Wilborn, Anderson, SC. *(SC Bureau of Vital Statistics, Certificate of Death, 1930 #9322.)*

P

PAGE, Alfred
Nichols c/o J. R. Battle Co., Marion County
Cook for 32nd Ga Regt under Gen. Riper, Capt. Sparks, Lt. Bolton, 2nd Lt. Kenney, Sgt. Walch, Sgt. Ware and Sgt. Covington
Served on Sullivans Island near Charleston 1862–1863
Applied 26 May 1923; approved 26 May 1923
Affidavit: Mrs. Elmira Page Johnson (niece of William J. Page of the 32nd Ga Regiment)
Application #8052: Alfred Page, married, laborer, 90 years old, died 13 June 1934 in Marion County. His wife was Alice Page. He was buried at Fortan. Informant—Grant Page, Nichols, SC. *(SC Bureau of VItal Statistics, Certificate of Death, 1934 #14536.)*

***PEARSON Warren**
Servant under James B. Fort, Co. E, 3rd Regt, State Troops, Capt. Bradley
Served eight to ten months

Members of an Augusta, Georgia, company with servant, May 1861. This company later became part of the 5th Georgia Regiment. Francis Trevelyan Miller, ed., ***The Photographic History of the Civil War,*** *vol. 10. (New York, The Review of Reviews Co., 1911).*

Source: List submitted by Thomas E. Richardson, judge of probate, Sumter County, 13 June 1923
Application #11276b

PITTS, Hessie
Chappells RFD, Newberry County
Cook and attendant under Washington Pitts, Co. B, 3rd Btn, Capt. John G. Williams
Served December 1861–26 April 1865
Applied 27 April 1923; approved 8 May 1923
Affidavits: R. T. Hollingsworth and W. B. Fuller
Application #8624

POINSETTE, Peter
26 [Hamilton] St, Charleston, Charleston County
Servant under Capt. B. H. Rutledge, Co. G, 4th Regt, SC Cav

Applied 17 March 1924; approved 23 March 1924
Affidavit: B. H. Rutledge
Application #1902

POLITE, Paul
Ridgeland, Jasper County
Servant under Capt. Manning Kirk, Kirks Squadron
Served 1864–1865
Applied 4 June 1923; approved 5 June 1923
Affidavits: Andrew Ford and John R. Stephenson
Application #6517: Paul Polite, married, farmer, 84 years 10 months old, died 13 May 1926 in Jasper County. He was the son of Susie Miner and Sam Polite and was born 19 June 1842. (*SC Bureau of Vital Statistics, Certificate of Death, 1926 #8784.)*

POLLOCK, John
Columbia, Richland County
Servant under D. L. Glenn, 12th regt, Capt. Harpie McMekin
Served 1861–1865
Applied 19 April 1923; approved 19 April 1923
Affidavits: D. L. Glenn and W. T. Glenn
Application #10160

POU, Louis
North, Orangeburg County
Servant under William Pou, Dantzler and Keitts Regts, and "regularly hauled supplies from the Livingston Mill at Beaver Creek for shipment to troops at Charleston. This mill was under control of Confederate Govmt."
Served "when war began"–"after close of war"
Applied 21 May 1923; approved 26 May 1923
Affidavits: A. F. Livingston and A. F. Porter. Mrs. Martha L. North, who was the daughter of Mary Pou and was too "ill and too feeble to sign," said Pou was her mother's servant.
Application #9436

POWER, Ben
Abbeville, Abbeville County
Cook under J. W. Power, Co. G, Capt. Johnson
Served June 1862–April 1865
Applied 19 April 1923; approved 19 April 1923
Application #156

PRINCE, Hiram
Cope, Orangeburg County

Servant under John F. Hartzog
Served from beginning of the war "off and on about nine months"
Applied 14 April 1923; approved 18 April 1923
Application #9440: Hiram Prince, married, 85 years old, died 11 February 1926 in Orangeburg County. He was buried at Cedar Grove. Informant—Willie Able, Cope, SC RFD. *(SC Bureau of Vital Statistics, Certificate of Death, 1926 #3006.)*

PRINGLE, Aaron, Sr.
Rhems Rt 1, Georgetown County
Servant under Capt. J. F. Carraway, Co. A, 10th Regt
Served 1861–1865
Applied 16 May 1923
Affidavit: H. W. Brewton
Application #4096: Aron Pringle, married, farmer, 95 years old, died 16 October 1929 in Georgetown County. He was the son of Rosa and Aron Pringle and was born in 1834. He was buried at Baloon. Informant—Isaac Pringle, Plantersville, SC. *(SC Bureau of Vital Statistics, Certificate of Death, 1929 #17557.)*

PROPHET, Frank
Perry, Aiken County
Servant under Capt. H. F. Salley
Served June 1864–January 1865
Applied 29 May 1923; approved 6 June 1923
Affidavit: U. P. Salley
Application #439: Frank Prophet, widower, 90 years old, died 29 March 1931 in Aiken County. He was buried at Antioch Church. Informant—L. E. Edwards, Wagener, SC. *(SC Bureau of Vital Statistics, Certificate of Death, 1931 #3368.)*

Q

QUARLES, Richard
Parksville RFD, McCormick County
Cook under Capt. Penion, Co. D, 14th Regt
Served January 1861–April 1865
Applied 7 May 1923; approved 7 May 1923
Affidavits: J. M. Mims and Joseph Brunson
Application #8204: Richard Quarles, widower, 85 years 6 months old, died 4 June 1925 in McCormick County. He was the son of Rebecca Bugg and George Quarles and was born 25 December 1835. He was buried at Mt. Mariah Church. Informant—Hugh Quarles, Plum Branch, SC. *(SC Bureau of Vital Statistics, Certificate of Death, 1925 #10284)*

QUARRELS, Hort
Vaucluse, Aiken County
Servant under G. W. Turner, Capt. Hard
Served January 1864–close of war 1865
Applied 15 May 1923; approved 15 May 1923
Affidavits: J. B. Leopard and T. G. Seager
Application #441

R

REAVES, Simuel
Mullins, Marion County
Laborer, Charleston fortifications
Application #8104

REED, Yancy
Abbeville, Abbeville County
Cook
Applied 19 May 1923; approved 19 May 1923
Application #164: Yancey Reid, married, retired farmer, 87 years old, died 10 December 1931 in Abbeville County. His wife was Jane Reid. He was the son of Adline Thomas and Yancey Reid and was buried in Harbison Cemetery, Abbeville, SC. Informant—Adline Jones, Abbeville, C. *(SC Bureau of Vital Statistics, Certificate of Death, 1931 #18823.)*

RENWICK, George Washington
Pomaria, Newberry County
Cook under George Lawson Co. D, 13th Regt, Capt. I. H. Hunt
Served 1861–April 1865
Applied 2 April 1923; approved 23 April 1923
Affidavits: George B. Aull and R. T. Caldwell
Application #8642

RHODES, Primus
Gray Court, Laurens County
Cook's attendant under Wiley Fowler, Co. E, 3rd Btn, Capt. W. H. Fowler
Served 1861–September 1863
Applied 24 April 1923; approved 3 May 1923
Affidavits: John W. Fowler and Mrs. S. E. Owens
Application #7275

RILLEY, William
Bowman, Orangeburg County
Servant under Milton Dantzler, Capt. Hagood
Served 1862–"surrender at Richmond, Va"
Applied 21 April 1923
Application #9448: William Rilley, married, farm laborer, 84 years old, died 23 May 1925 in Orangeburg County. He was born in 1841 and was buried at Rocky Hill. Informant—Ed Rillers, Bowman, SC. *(SC Bureau of Vital Statistics, Certificate of Death, 1925 #8481.)*

RING, Frank
Greenville, Greenville County
Servant under Capt. Maffett, Co. C, 3rd Regt
Served April 1861 until "he returned home with his master."
Applied 2 January 1924
Affidavits: A. B. Cromer and William Y. Fair
Application #5608

RIVERS, Josiah
Ehrhardt, Bamberg County
Laborer under I. S. Bamberg, Co. C, 1st Regt
Entered service May 1862
Applied 8 May 1923; approved 8 May 1923
Affidavits: J. C. Copeland and J. I. Copeland
Application #1266: Josiah Rivers, married, farmer, about 84 years old, died 15 September 1923 in Bamberg County. He was the son of Bettie Johnston and Sam Rivers. *(SC Bureau of Vital Statistics, Certificate of Death, 19232 #13909.)*

ROCHE, Aaron
Abbeville, Abbeville County
Attendant to Capt. Partlow
Served 1862–end of war 1865
Applied 31 May 1923; approved 2 June 1923
Application #166

RUFF, Sancho
c/o Mrs. J. C. B. Smith, Colonial Heights, Columbia, Richland County
Servant under Lt. D. W. Ruff, Co. C, 2nd Regt Cav, Capt. Hampton, Col. Meigham
Served 1861–11 April 1865
Applied 11 April 1923; approved 19 April 1923
Affidavit: J. P. Rawls
Application #10185

William Rose, servant of Gen. Maxcy Gregg. Rose is wearing General Gregg's uniform, which Gregg gave to Rose. Gregg died 13 December 1862 following the Battle of Fredericksburg, Va. SC Cnfederate Relic Room and Museum.

S

SAMPSON, John
Bishopville, Lee County
Cook under Capt. Shavers, Capt. Cason
Served 1862–April 1865
Applied 23 April 1923; approved 24 May 1923
Affidavits: Sarah I. Smith and Mrs. S. O. Mathis
Application #7517: John Sampson, widowed, 84 years old, died 6 February 1924 in Lee County. He was buried at Bethlehem Church. Informant—Ned Wilson, Bishopville, SC. *(SC Bureau of Vital Statistics, Certificate of Death, 1924 #2807).*

***SANDERS, Alpheus**
Servant under Lt. and Capt. Samuel M. Richardson, White's Bttn Artillery
Served two years and then "sent home to nurse old Capt. Jno S. Richardson father of Col. Jno S. Richardson . . . "

Source: List submitted by Thomas E. Richardson, judge of probate, Sumter County, 13 June 1923
Application #11276b

SANDERS, John Milton
Whitmire, RFD #1, Newberry County
Cook under William Stone, Co. A, 13th Regt, Capt. R. L. Bowden
Served 6 August 1861–1 December 1863
Applied 2 May 1923; approved 11 May 1923
Affidavits: James Denson and S. P. McCrackin
Application #8656: John Sanders, married, farmer/day laborer, 80 years old, died 2 April 1925 in Newberry County. He was born in 1845 and was the son of Chattie and Meton Sanders. He was buried at Bush River. Informant—Lizza Sanders, RFD #1, Kinards, SC. *(SC Bureau of Vital Statistics, Certificate of Death, 1925 #6404.)*

SANDERS, William
Blackville, Barnwell County
Servant to Dr. J. B. Baxley, surgeon in charge of 3rd Georgia Hospital, Augusta, Georgia
Served 1863–end of war
Applied 23 April 1923; approved 24 April 1923
Affidavits: J. V. Baxley and L. F. Hair
Application #1470

SAUNDERS, William
Fort Motte, Calhoun County
Cook under Thomas Jones, Black's Regiment, Capt. Johnson
Served 6 August 1861–3 April 1865
Applied 24 April 1923
Affidavits: John W. Scott, W. L. Duckett, and H. H. C. [Paulling]
Application #1715

SCOTT, Caesar
Sheldon, Beaufort County
Servant under John Oswald, Co. K, 3rd Regt, Capt. William Peeples
Served 1861–1864
Approved 31 March 1924
Affidavits: William R. Stone and George W. Tuten
Application #1544: Caeser Scott, widowed, farmer, 88 years old, died 28 February 1928 in Beaufort County. He was the son of Frank Scott and was buried in Sa[—] Cemetery. Informant—Treuell Scott, Sheldon, SC. *(SC Bureau of Vital Statistics, Certificate of Death, 1928 #3913.)*

SEASE, Louis
Ehrhardt, Bamberg County
Laborer under W. E. Sease, Co. C, 1st Regt, Capt. I. S. Bamberg
Served 1862
Applied 8 May 1923; approved 8 May 1923
Affidavits: J. C. Copeland and J. I. Copeland
Application #1272

SIMMONS, Wylie
Allendale, Allendale County
Cook under Capt. Dickenson, Co. G, 17th Regt
Served October 1861–April 1865
Applied 10 May 1923; approved 11 May 1923
Affidavits: H. M. Goodson and Dr. J. M. Weekley
Application #623

SINGLETON, Benjamin
Beaufort, Beaufort County
Servant under Capt. John H. Thompson, Co. E, 1st Regt
His statement: "I served under Capt. Thompson until after the second battle Manassas, in which he was killed. I was then transferred to Beaufort Volunteer Artillery and served under Sergt. Wm. Thompson, Corporal David Thompson, until after the battle of Honey Hill. Was then transferred to the batallion from the Citadel Academy and Columbia school Boys, under Robert and James Thompson, and served until the close of the war when I was discharged at Greenville, S. C."
Served May 1, 1861–close of war, 1865
Applied 26 December 1923
Affidavits: Robert Thomson (Washington, D. C.) and Annie M. Furse
Application #1547: Benjamin Singleton, widowed, carpenter, 79 years old, died 15 August 1926 in Beaufort County. The son of Grace Myers, he was buried in Beaufort. *(SC Bureau of Vital Statistics, Certificate of Death, 1926 #44057.)*

SINGLETON, James
St. Stephen, Berkeley County
Servant and cook, Hampton's Brigade, 6th Regt, Capt. Humphrey
Served four years until 1865
Applied 27 April 1923; approved 30 April 1923
Affidavit: F. N. Schipman, former owner
Application #1653

SMALL, Elisha
Murrells Inlet, Horry County

African American musicians entertained Confederate and Federal troops. Lightfoot Collection.

Cook under Capt. Josh Ward, Ward's Art
Served 1861
Approved 10 April 1923
Affidavit: J. H. Jollie
Application #6428

SMITH, Frank
Bamberg, Bamberg County
Servant under David Jimerson, Co. B, Hagood's Regt, Capt. Samelton
Served March 1861–end of war
Applied 6 April 1923; approved 7 April 1923
Affidavits: A. R. Dempsey and R. C. Dempsey
Application #1274: Frank Smith, widowed, farmer, about 82 years old, died 12

December 1927 in Bamberg County. He was the son of Isabella Jamison and Adam Smith and was buried in Midway Cemetery. Informant—Dave Smith, Bamberg, SC. (*SC Bureau of Vital Statistics, Certificate of Death, 1927 #19543.)*

SMITH, John R.
Fair Play, Oconee County
Cook and attendant under William Smith and Jesse Smith, 4th Regt, Rutledge Mounted Rifles, Capt. Claudius E. Earle. Smith also worked part of the time on the breastworks around Charleston.
Served 1861–December 1864
Applied 10 May 1923; approved 12 May 1923
Affidavit: J. R. Earle, based upon information he received from his father, J. R. Earle, and Martin Smith, father of the soldiers mentioned.
Application #9105

SPEED, Luke
Lowndesville, Abbeville County
Servant under Capt. White
Applied 10 May 1923; approved 10 May 1923
Application #182

SPENCER, George
Abbeville RFD #4, Abbeville County
Cook under Ben Harvely
Served until end of war
Applied 14 April 1923; approved 14 April 1923
Application #184

***STENHOUSE, Wash**
Fountain Inn, Greenville County
Servant under John Taylor Stenhouse, son of his master, Adam Stenhouse
Served during 1861 until John Taylor Stenhouse was mortally wounded in the first battle and died at Culpepper, Virginia
Source: L. L. Thomason, Mrs. W. S. Redin (grand-daughter of Adam Stenhouse) and J. D. McKittrick and Mrs. M. J. Sprouse (Adam Stenhouse's nephew and niece.) McKittrick and Sprouse said they had known Wash Stenhouse for 57 years, that he had been married when they first knew him, and that they estimated his age in 1923 to be 78.
Application #5663

STOKER, Bill
Bamberg, Bamberg County
Cook under F. C. Ayer, Kirks' Squad, Capt. Kirk

Served 1863–end of war
Applied 12 May 1923; approved 12 May 1923
Affidavits: L. M. Ayer and P. M. Varn
Application #1289

STUART, Dock
Williston, Barnwell County
Cook under Sullivan Weathersbee, Co. A, 1st Regt, SCV, Capt. Wick McCreary
Served June 1863–April 1865
Applied 15 May 1923; approved 16 May 1923
Affidavits: L. H. Hair and J. A. Meyer
Application #1472

SULLIVAN, Milton
Greenwood, Greenwood County
Servant under Charles Moseley, Co. B, Orrs Regt, Capt. Perrin
Served 1 March 1863–15 April 1865
Applied 5 April 1923; approved 7 May 1923
Affidavits: J. F. Davis and C. R. Calhoun. Note: Calhoun signed based upon information he had heard from his father, C. W. Calhoun.
Application #6031

SUMTER, Stepney
Hampton, Hampton County
Servant under Capt. Spann, Beaufort Art "waiting on - - - Tommy Spann on S. C. Coast."
Served 1861–surrender 1865
Applied 9 January 1924; approved 9 January 1924
Affidavits: none; all known are dead. Board of Honor believed Sumter's statement.
Application #6193: Stepney Sumter, married, laborer, 80 years 6 months and 4 days old, died 4 July 1924 in Hampton County. Born in Beaufort County, he was buried in Bethlehem Cemetery. Informant—Jim Reid, Hampton, SC. *(SC Bureau of Vital Statistics, Certificate of Death, 1924 #13001.)*

SWINTON, Paul
Eutawville c/o Willie Gilliard, Orangeburg County
Servant under H. M. Palmer, Marion Light Artillery Battery, Capt. Parker
Served 1862–close of war 1865
Applied 6 April 1923; approved 18 April 1923
Affidavit: H. B. Kirk. Kirk certified that Paul Swinton served as a servant to his master H. M. Palmer, now deceased.
Application #9501: Paul Swinton, widowed, laborer, about 80 years old, died 12 January 1930 in Orangeburg County. He was buried in [Poplar] Hill. Informant—

Ben Goodson, Eutawville, SC. *(SC Bureau of Vital Statistics, Certificate of Death, 1930 #1170.)*

T

THOMAS, Benjamin
North Augusta, Aiken County
Cook, Co. I, 2nd Regt, Capt. M. C. Butler
Served May 1861–April 1865
Applied 5 April 1912; approved 22 May 1923
Affidavit: H. E. Mealing and J. M. Glover. Glover said Mealing was the only survivor of the company, but he knew that Ben Thomas belonged to his father M. O. Glover, a member of that company
Application #494

THOMAS, Charles
Branchville, Orangeburg County
Servant under Judge (Capt.) J. F. Izlar
Served 1862–close of war 1865
Applied 6 May 1924; approved 16 May 1924
Affidavit: Daniel W. Byrd
Application #9503: Charles Thomas, married, laborer, 80 years old, died 28 December 1927 in Orangeburg County. He was buried in Canaan Cemetery. Informant—Dave Williams, Branchville, SC. *(SC Bureau of Vital Statistics, Certificate of Death, 1927 #20966.)*

THOMPSON, Lavina (female, 78 years)
Salley RFD #2 c/o R. B. Thompson, Aiken County
Cook under Sam Webb, Co. A, 1st Regt Reserves, Capt. Hutto
Served 1 September 1863–end of war 1865
Applied 11 May 1923; approved 15 May 1923
Affidavits: Harrison Davis (75 years) and Jane Anderson (73 years)
Application #496

TILLEY, James Irvin
Cameron, Calhoun County
Servant and laborer under William Gaffney, Capt. Humbert. Laborer on fortifications on James Island and Johns Island
Served October 1865–20 April 1866
Applied 26 April 1923

African American scouts, winter, 1864–1865, City Point, Va. Library of Congress LC-B811-2676.

Affidavits: E. P. Haigler and P. D. Tilley
Application #1721

TILLMAN, Ruben
Trenton, Edgefield County
Cook under J. Monroe Wise, Co. I, 2nd Regt SC Cav, Capt. M. C. Butler
Served 1861–1865
Applied 14 April 1923
Affidavit: Walter Wise said his father, 1st Sgt. J. Monroe Wise, served in Co. I, 2nd SC Cav, Capts. M. C. Butler, T. H. Clark, and J. J. Bunch, and that Rubin Tillman was his father's cook and servant.
Application #3625

TOMPKINS, Mat
Modoc, McCormick County

Servant under Bob and Capt. Gus Tompkins, Co. B, Hampton Legion
Served beginning–end of war
Applied 13 April 1923; approved 15 April 1923
Affidavits: W. J. Talbert and James B. Tompkins
Application # 8229

TOWNSEND, Doctor
Bennettsville RFD, Marlboro County
Cook, Co. G, 8th Regt, Capt. C. P. Townsend
Served May 1861–December 1861
Applied 21 April 1923; approved 24 April 1923
Affidavits: C. P. Townsend and Jack R. Stubbs
Application #8397: Doc Townsend, widower, 86 years old, died 17 July 1923 in Marlboro County. He was the son of Mary and Henry Townsend and was buried in Smyrna Cemetery. Informant—Robert Stewart, Bennettsville, SC. *(SC Bureau of Vital Statistics, Certificate of Death, 1923 #11616.)*

TUCKER, Sam
Iva, Abbeville County
Cook under T. A. Calir et al, Co. I, 14th Regt, Capt. William White
Served June 1863–April 1865
Applied 11 April 1923; approved 11 April 1923
Affidavits: J. B. Hampton and M. W. Barns
Application #197

V

VAUSE, Elvin
Due West, Abbeville County
Cook under Lt. Ben Roper, Co. I, 7th Regt, Capt. William Prescot
Served 1861–April 1865
Applied 16 April 1923; approved 18 April 1923
Affidavits: M. E. Holingsworth and R. H. McAdams
Application #212: Elvin Vauss, married, brick mason, 84 years old, died 17 January 1929 in Abbeville County. He was the son of Edna Vauss and was buried at Mt. Lebanon. *(SC Bureau of Vital Statistics, Certificate of Death, 1929 #0017.)*

VEREEN, Wesley
Rhems, Georgetown County
Servant under J. Bellune, Co. F, 7th SC Cav, Capt. McDaniel

Served 3 August 1861–July 1862
Applied 15 May 1923
Affidavit: J. J. Johnson
Application #4108

W

WALKER, Jerry
Blackville, Barnwell County
Servant under Capt. R. M. Willis, Co. D, 2nd Regt
Served 1 November 1864–1 May 1865
Applied 7 May 1923; approved 21 May 1923
Affidavits: M. W. Phillips and L. F. Hair
Application #1487

WALKER, Peter
Orangeburg, Orangeburg County
Servant under Tom Oliver, 25th Regt, Capt. J. F. Izlar
Served over six months
Applied 18 April 1923; approved 18 April 1923
Affidavits: Elvira Whittimore and Joe McNamara. Both said Peter Walker served with his master, Tom Oliver.
Application #9511: Peter Walker, married, laborer, 88 years old, died 19 July 1925 in Orangeburg County. He was the son of Patsey and Scipio Walker and was buried at Jersusalem M. E. Church. Informant—Marion Walker, Orangeburg, SC. *(SC Bureau of Vital Statistics, Certificate of Death, 1925 #12405)*

WALLACE, Marshall
Newberry, Newberry County
Servant under Samuel W. Spearman, Co. C, Holcombe Legion, Capt. Robert Spearman
Served September 1861–April 1865
Applied 12 January 1924; approved 2 April 1924
Affidavits: F. G. Spearman and William Y. Fair
Application #8703

WASHINGTON, Daniel
Orangeburg County
Servant under Patrick P. Jennings, Harts Battery, Washington Artillery, Capt. Tyler
Served 1861–surrendered at Richmond

Applied 14 April 1923; approved 16 April 1923
Affidavits: J. A. McCormack and W. B. Smoak
Application #1297

WIGFALL, Sank
North Augusta, Aiken County
Cook under G. A. Adams, Gen. Freyer's command, Capt. H. W. Shaw
Served about March 1864–end of war 1865
Applied 7 April 1924; approved 23 April 1924
Affidavits: George B. Anderson and G. A. Adams
Application #516

***WIGGINS, CARY**
Marion RFD #1, Marion County
Laborer, fortifications at Charleston
Approved 26 May 1923 by Marion County Board of Honor
Application #8104

WIGGINS, Harrison
Seneca, Oconee County
Servant under Ransom Calhoun and Capt. Teddy Calhoun, Co. A, Lucas Btn
Served April 1861–1864
Applied 19 May 1923; approved 20 May 1923
Affidavits: A. W. Elrod and G. W. Gignilliat. Gignilliat said he had known Harrison Wiggins forty years and "found him honest and prompt in the discharge of his obligations, faithful to any trust imposed on him."
Application #9138: Harrison Wiggins, widowed, retired farmer, 88 years 9 months old, died 4 June 1929 in Oconee County. Born in September 1840, he was buried in Nebo, SC. Informant—S. H. Knox, Seneca, SC. *(SC Bureau of Vital Statistics, Certificate of Death, 1929 #10809.)*

WILKINS, Pinkney
Landrum, Spartanburg County
Cook under Capt. Sam Snoddy, 7th Regt
Served 1863–end of war 1865
Applied 1 May 1923; approved 24 May 1923
Affidavits: J. C. Wilkins and C. W. Wilkins
Application #11088

WILLIAMS, Alex
Due West, Abbeville County
Cook under Dr. Henry Klugh, Capt. White
Served 1864–1865

Applied 14 May 1923; approved 14 May 1923
Application #206
Alexander Williams, a widowed farmer, 75, died 30 January 1924 in Abbeville County. Wiliams was the son of Helen Tate and Miles Williams and was born 16 July 1849. He was buried in Friendship Cemetery. Informant—Alice Latimer, Honea Path, Rt 3. *(SC Bureau of Vital Statistics, Certificate of Death, 1924 #12.)*

WILLIAMS, Alex
Jackson, Aiken County
Servant under J. Foreman and B. Foreman, Co. C, 1st Regt, SC Cav, Capts. Twiggs and Brown
Served 27 August 1861–26 April 1865
Applied 8 May 1923; approved 15 May 1923
Affidavits: John H. Hankinson, Jr., and W. F. Green, Sr.
Application #517

WILLIAMS, Ambrose
Helena, Newberry County
Servant under Richard Chalmers, Co. A, 1st Cav Regt, Capt. Owens
Served 1862–August 1864
Applied 16 April 1923; approved 23 April 1923
Affidavits: R. Y. Leavell and William Y. Fair
Application #8728

WILLIAMS, Bram
Allendale, Allendale County
Cook under Capt. H. C. Stuart, Co. F, 3rd Regt, SC Cav
Served 1862–1865
Applied 28 May 1923; approved 28 May 1923
Affidavits: H. C. Weekley and J. C. McMillan
Application #634: Bram Williams, married, farmer, 87 years old, died 30 August 1927 in Allendale County. He was buried in Hoover Cemetery. *(SC Bureau of Vital Statistics, Certificate of Death, 1927 #12466.)*

WILLIAMS, Green
Eastover, Richland County
Laborer under Capt. Alex Haskell
Served until the war ended
Applied 30 April 1923; approved 8 May 1923
Affidavits: T. Stark House and P. House
Application #10261: Green Williams, married, farmer, 82 years old, died 16 July 1923 in Richland County. Born in 1841, he was the son of Phoebe and William

African American teamsters, 1864. Brady Collection, Library of Congress.

Williams. He was buried at Mt. Zion Church. Informant—Henry Williams, Eastover, SC. *(SC Bureau of Vital Statistics, Certificate of Death, 1923 #11906.)*

WILLIAMS, Henry
Taylors, Rt 1, Greenville County
Salt maker under Capt. William Hoy, Charleston
Applied 12 May 1923
Affidavit: Mrs. J. H. Brockman and Alfred P. Hoy. Brockman and Hoy said Henry Williams belonged to their father, Maj. William Hoy, and worked at the Charleston salt works. Hoy and his workers "stayed too long at the salt works and were overtaken by Sherman's army between Charleston and Lancaster."
Application #5762

WILLSON, James
Westminister, Oconee County
Cook under Capt. Langston, 16th Regt
Served 1862–1864
Applied 20 April 1923; approved 12 May 1923
Affidavits: Ira S. Pitts and Oscar W. Pitts said that according to their father, Willson served.
Application #9143

WILSON, Hammett
Spring Street, Spartanburg, Spartanburg County
Servant under John P. May, Co. D, 3rd Btn, Capt. G. M. Gunnels and Capt. John N. Harris
Served November 1861–May 1865
Applied 10 April 1923; approved 16 April 1923
Affidavits: John P. May and R. J. Copeland, Sr. May said Hamett Wilson served with him.
Applicaton #11101: Hammit Wilson, married, laborer, 100, died 25 March 1928 in Spartanburg County. Born in 1828, he was the son of Julia Wilson and Larken Burnside. He was buried in Laurens, SC. Informant—Berthia Wilson, Spartanburg, SC. *(SC Bureau of Vital Statistics, Certificate of Death, 1928 #5412.)*

WILSON, Mart
Clinton RFD, Laurens County
Cook and attendant under J. H. Copeland, Co. B, 1st Regt, SC Cav, Capt. Nesbitt
Served more than six months
Applied 4 May 1923; approved 9 May 1923
Affidavits: J. W. Peterson and George Wilson
Application #7365

WILSON, Martin
Laurens, Laurens County
Servant and cook under J. H. Copland and Joseph Little, Co. B, 1st Regt, SC Cav, Capt. Nesbitt
Served more than twelve months
Applied 8 May 1923; approved 8 May 1923
Affidavits: J. C. Davis and Nelson Vance
Application #7366

***WILSON, Robert**
Sumter County
Servant under Lt. B. F. Wilson
Served: entire war
Source: List submitted by Thomas E. Richardson, judge of probate, Sumter County, 13 June 1923
Application #11270b

WILSON, Squire
Laurens, Laurens County
Cook and attendant under A. W. Teague, Co. A, 3rd Regt, SC Inf, Capt. B. C. Washington

Served 15 April 1861–25 April 1865
Applied 19 April 1923; approved 19 April 1923
Affidavits: T. S. Langston and Mel Fleming
Application #7368: Squire Wilson, about 87 years old, died 21 February 1930 in Laurens County. He was the son of Judy Wilson and Julie Young (father) and was a resident of the county home when he died. He was buried in Rocky Spring. Informant—J. Chatman, Laurens, SC. (*SC Bureau of Vital Statistics, Certificate of Death, 1930 #2611.)*

WINGATE, G. Wash
Cheraw, Chesterfield County
Cook under Capt. T. E. Powe, Co. C, 8th Regt
Served October 1861–October 1863
Applied 6 April 1923; approved 7 April 1923
Affidavit: G. A. Malloy
Application #2613

WINN, George
Abbeville, Abbeville County
Cook, Capt. Youngblood
Served June 1862–April 1865
Applied 30 May 1923
Application #211

WISE, Ben
Columbia, Richland County
Cook under Capt. George Swygert, Co. A, 3rd Regt, Kershaws Brigade
Served fall 1861–end of war 1865
Applied 13 April 1923; approved 12 April 1923
Affidavit: L. W. Taylor
Application #10271: Ben Wise, widowed, carpenter, 75 years old, died 21 February 1925 in Richland County. He was born in 1849 and was buried in Randoph Cemetery. Informant—SC State Hospital Record. *(SC Bureau of Vital Statistics, Certificate of Death, 1925 #2836.)*

WISE, Lewis
Blackville, Barnwell County
Cook under Capt. S. Wise, Co. A, 3rd Regt, SC Cav, Capt. Kirkland
Served one year
Applied 21 April 1923; approved 21 May 1923
Affidavits: Capt. John Wise and L. H. Hair
Application #1497

WOODSON, Caleb
Edgewood, Richland County
Laborer
Served over six months
Applied 8 April 1923; approved 8 May 1923
Affidavits: James M. Gee and Caleb Woodson
Application #10272: Caleph Woodson, married, farmer, 85 years old, died 18 April 1925 in Richland County. The son of Henry Woodson, he was buried at Gill Creek. Informant—Sam Woodson, Edgewood Post Office, SC. *(SC Bureau of Vitsal Statistics, Certificate of Death, 1925 #6660.)*

WRIGHT, Johnson
Seneca, Oconee County
Cook under Capt. Kilpatrick, Co. K, Palmetto Sharpshooters
Served 1862 until death of Capt. Kilpatrick in 1864
Applied 20 April 1923; approved 12 May 1923
Affidavits: S. K. Dendy and W. D. Stribling
Application #9144: Johnson Wright, widowed, retired farmer, about 100 years old, died 12 March 1825 in Oconee County. He was buried at Old Zion Church. Informant—David Brown, Seneca, SC. *(SC Bureau of Vital Statistics, Certificate of Death, 1925 #4476)*

Y

YOUMANS, John
Hampton, Hampton County
Cook under Swift Hubbard, 3rd Regt, SC Cav, Capt. Howard
served 1861–1865
Applied 17 May 1923; approved 14 May 1923
Application #6211

YOUNG, Isaac
White Oak, Fairfield County
Cook under John Young, Co. B, 4th Regt, Capt. Osbon Barber
Served two years and six months
Applied 16 April 1924
Application #3808

***YOUNG, J. M.**
Abbeville, Abbeville County
Cook under J. W. Thomas

Served 1863–1864
Applied 10 May 1923; approved 10 May 1923
Application #216

YOUNG, Limus
Holly Hill, Orangeburg County
Cook, servant, and teamster under William Bull, Capts. Elias Venning and Fred Schultz
Served October 1863–end of war 1865 (discharged Hillsboro, North Carolina)
Applied 2 May 1923; approved 26 May 1923.
Affidavits: John M. Shingler and J. L. Smith
Application #9543: Lymus Young, widower, 77 years old, died 5 November 1928 in Orangeburg County. He was buried in Bruier Graveyard. Informant—Matthew Stoutamire, Holly Hill, SC. *(SC Bureau of Vital Statistics, Certificate of Death, 1928 #20548.)*

YOUNG, Ross
Laurens, Laurens County
Laborer under Hydrick (overseer), sea island fortifications
Served more than six months
Applied 7 May 1923; approved 8 May 1923
Affidavits: Cinda Young and Henry Montgomery
Application #7378: Ross Young, widower, 83 years old, died 26 October 1925 in Laurens County. He was buried at Poplar Springs. Informant—John Elmore, Laurens, SC. *(SC Bureau of Vital Statistics, Certificate of Death, 1925 #17404.)*

Pensioners Noah Johnson and Ben Wise were buried in Randolph Cemetery, Columbia, S.C. National Register files, State Historic Preservation Office, SCDAH.

Appendix A—Nina L. Brown

An interesting sidelight to the search for African American Confederate pensioners is the application of Nina L. Brown. Brown, the widow of R. Sebastian Brown, filed for a pension under the Act of 1919. Her application, dated 26 April 1919, said her husband had served under Capt. James Span in Co. G, Hampton's Legion and in Co. K, 7th Regiment, SC Cavalry. R. Sebastian Brown died 18 January 1918. The Browns were married on 15 June 1879. In 1919, the widow, aged 69, lived near Rembert in Sumter County.

What separated this application from the hundreds of other applications for Confederate pensions in South Carolina was the race of the widow. The South Carolina Attorney General rendered the following opinion on 23 May 1919:

> "the widow to whom you refer having been the reputed wife of a man who served as a soldier in the confederate army, will be entitled to a pension, under the Act of the recent General Assembly, provided, of course, her marriage was consummated on the 15th day of June, of the year, 1879, as the Act prohibiting such marriages was not approved until December 12th, of that year."[1]

Nina Brown, a widowed housekeeper, died 22 January 1925. Her death certificate listed Agnes Saunders as her mother. E. W. Saunders, Rembert, SC., provided the information. She was buried in Pisgah 12 January 1925.[2]

---

1. Records of the South Carolina Comptroller General, Applications for Confederate Pension, 1919-1926, Application #1148 a and b. Act no. 5 (1879) prohibited miscegenation in South Carolina.
2. SC Bureau of Vital Statistics, Certificate of Death, 1925, #8860.

Appendix B—Comptroller General's list

In his 1926 report to the General Assembly, the comptroller general, for the first time, listed the African American Confederate pensioners individually. It is reproduced below and preserves the spelling of the original. Applications do not exist at the state level for all pensioners.

Abbeville County
Black, Jeff
Bugg, Jim
Frazier, Marcus
Jackson, Dennis
Jones, Henry
McAllister, Andrew
McClinton, Jack
Noble, Isaac
Power, Ben
Reid, Yance
Roche, Aaron
Tucker, Sam
Vauss, Elvin
Willard, Henry
Williams, Harry

Aiken County
Barrett, Emmett, *Aiken*
Gass, Elliott, *North Augusta*
Gantt, Will, *North Augusta*
Harrison, Alex, *Aiken R.F.D. 2*
Kelly, Ansell, *Jackson*
Neal, Charlie, *Aiken*
Prophet, Frank, *Perry*
Quarles, Hort, *Vaucluse*
Thompson, Lavinia, *Salley*
Wigfall, Sank, *North Augusta*
Williams, Alex, *Jackson*

Allendale County
DeLoach, Richard, *Allendale*
Goodwin, Joe, *Barton*
Jemerson, Aaran, *Allendale*
Loadholt, Miles, *Ulmers*
Robinson, Solomon, *Sycamore*
Smith, Harry, *Allendale*
Williams, Bram, *Sycamore*

Anderson County
Childs, Wade
Mattison, Marshall
Owens, Starling

Bamberg County
Felder, Henry
Gold, Sam
Smith, Frank
Stokes, Bill
Whitmire, Henry

Barnwell County
Anderson, Burkett
Best, Ben
Brister, Comedore
Brown, Anderson
Chance, Lloyd
Daniels, Marchus
Dunbar, Boston
Floyd, Henry
Gantt, Edd
Geter, Peter
Givins, George
Gothers, Sandy
Greene, Charles
Jackson, Lewis
Keel, Daniel
Stewart, Dock
Walker, Jerry
Wise, Lewis

Beaufort County
Alston, Richard, *Bluffton*
Bolds, Samuel, *Beaufort*
Scott, Caesar, *Beaufort*

Berkeley County
Johnson, Harry, *Cross Hill*

Charleston County
Campbell, Paul, *James Island*
Collins, Jim, *Charleston*
Drayton, Isaac, *Charleston*
Ladson, S. W., *Adams Run*
Lewis, W. S., *Charleston*
Mack, Daniel, *Edisto Island*
Middleton, Louis, *Charleston*
Mikell, Wallace, *Charleston*
Poinsett, Peter, *Charleston*
Steed, John, *Awendaw*

Cherokee County
Corry, Jake, *Gaffney*
Fewell, Samuel, *Blacksburg*
Littlejohn, Elijah, *Gaffney*
White, George, *Gaffney*

Chester County
Archer, Reuben
Bowser, Nathan
Caldwell, Gilbert
Crawford, Scott
Edwards, Ned
Feaster, Jerry
Feaster, Robert
Gaston, James
Jordan, Luke
Lightener, Frank
Pratt, Hugh
Ross, Henry
Williams, James

Chesterfield County
Ellerbe, Isaac
Green, Jacob
Hudley, Henry
Rivers, Joseph
Wingate, G. Wash

Clarendon County
Johnson, William
Wheeler, Joseph

Colleton County
Crosby, Isaac
Franklin, Jerry D.
Grantham, John
Harrison, Joe
Martin, W. M.
Rice, Sarah

Darlington County
Anderson, Cato, *Darlington*
Bacot, Mitchell, *Society Hill*
Canon, Marcus, *Darlington*
Coleman, Fred, *Darlington*
Dennis, Henry, *Darlington*
Field, Joe, *Darlington*
Frasier, Henry, *Hartsville*
Keith, Ferdinand, *Darlington*
McLendon, Curtis, *Darlington*
Pooler, J. B., *Darlington*
Smith, Enoch, *Darlington*
Timmons, Harry, *Society Hill*

Dillon County
Carmichael, Elijah
Davis, Stephens
Grice, Joe

Dorchester County
Bunch, Simon
Jenkins, Esaw
Johnson, Hector
Lee, Jacob
Simmons, Joe

Edgefield County
Byrd, Cain, *Edgefield*
Dean, Aaron, *Edgefield*
Hart, Tillman, *Johnston*
Martin, William, *Edgefield*

Fairfield County
Boulware, Ed, *Shelton*
Brown, Zack, *Woodward*
Coleman, Wm. P., *Shelton*
Craig, Sam, *Winnsboro*
David, Henry, *Blairs*
Egleston, Sam, *Winnsboro*
Mobley, Harrison, *Winnsboro*

Moore, Hiram, *Winnsboro*
Sawyer, Luke, *Winnsboro*

Florence County
Anderson, Friday
Beon, Joe B.
Brown, Leonard
Davis, Beverly
Edwards, Bright
Garland, Prince
Hinds, Smart
Ison, Isaac
John, Jack
Kelly, Carolina
Laney, Isaac
Lee, Isaac
Robinson, Lewis
Sanders, Sallie
Sims, Alford
Singetary, Evander
Sparks, Simon
Small, George
Stephenson, Olive
Sweet, Tom
Thames, John
Thomas, J. T.
Wilson, Simon

Georgetown County
Avery, John
Brown, Quakoo
Cooper, Amus
Ford, Edwin P.
Ford, Frederick
Ford, Henry James
Gasque, John
Hardee, Derry
Lawrence, Esau
Moultrie, Shederick
Pringle, Aaron
Smith, Madison
Vareen, Wesley

Greenville County
Abercrombie, Edom
Abercrombie, Silas
Clardy, Yancy
Davis, Nelson
Dawkins, Mallery
Garrett, Robert
Gentry, Samuel
Gray, George
Keith, Elias
Rector, Will
Ring, Peter
Stenhouse, Wash
Walker, Thomas

Greenwood County
Bowie, Jefferson
Butler, Ed
Chappell, Ben
Christie, Sam
Cohen, Abram
Dean, Elias
Harrison, Warren
Hearst, Wesley
Hodges, George
Howard, Stephen
Hutchinson, Charlie
Jackson, Griffith
Logan, West
Makin, Matthew
Sullivan, Milton
Washington, Will

Hampton County
Bing, Tom, *Furman*
Campbell, Tom, *Brunson*
Datta, Lazarus, *Estill*
Ginn, Ransom, *Hampton*
Haynes, Jenkins, *Brunson, R-1*
McTeer, Caesar, *Hampton*
Youmans, John, *Hampton*

Jasper County
Laurell, Bill, *Pineland*

Kershaw County
Boykin, Henry
Drakeford, Wash

Lancaster County
Barnes, Robert
Blakeney, Alfred
Clyburn, Joe

Laurens County
Adair, Alfred, *Renno*
Barksdale, Wash, *Barksdale*
Conway, Lonnie, *Cross Hill*
Franks, Ben, *Fountain Inn*
Fuller, Dan, *Waterloo*
Henry, Addison, *Laurens*
Hunter, Tom, *Ora*
Rhodes, Primus, *Gray Court*
Watts, Anthony, *Cross Hill*
Wilson, Mart, *Clinton*
Wilson, Martin, *Laurens*
Wilson, Squire, *Laurens*

Lee County
Bristow, McDonald
Daniels, Jake
Oliver, Solomon

Lexington County
Dennis, Wesley, *Leesville*
Hartley, Robert, *Batesburg*
Johnson, Albert, *Irmo*
Jones, Isiah, *Lexington*
Jones, Jackson, *Swansea*
Moseley, Ed, *Leesville*

McCormick County
Alfred, T. M.
Brown, Nelson
Mims, Dallas
Tompkins, Mat

Marion County
Donnelly, Ben, *Marion*
Franklin, Trus, *Marion*
Miller, Berry, *Latta*
Page, Alfred, *Nichols*

Newberry County
Cannon, Josh, *Newberry*
Haltiwanger, Abe, *Newberry*
Mitchell, Theodore, *Pomaria*
Pitts, Hessie, *Chappells*
Renwick, George, *Pomaria*
Sanders, John M., *Whitmire*
Wallace, Marshall, *Newberry*
Williams, Ambrose, *Helena*

Oconee County
Cherry, J. E., *Seneca*
Crayton, Jacob, *Walhalla*
Wiggins, Harrison, *Seneca*
Wilson, James, *Westminster*

Orangeburg County
Baxter, Charles, *Rowesville*
Burgess, William T., *Elloree*
Clark, Henry, *Orangeburg*
Grover, Frank, *Vance*
Holmes, Gilbert, *Orangeburg*
Jenkins, Nelson, *Norway*
Jones, William, *Orangeburg*
Lawton, Charles, *Orangeburg*
McLeod, John, *North*
Mitchell, June, *Orangeburg*
Swinton, Paul, *Eutawville*
Washington, Daniel W., *Elloree*
Young, Limus C., *Holly Hill*

Richland County
Able, Anderson, *Richland County*
Chapman, General, *Irmo*
Hinton, Joseph, *Eastover*
Johnson, Noah, *Columbia*
McDonald, Bob, *State Park*
Pollock, John, *Richland County*
Ruff, Sancho, *Columbia*
Williams, Charles, *Richland County*

Saluda County
Clary, Santaanna
Hill, Adam
Mobley, Richmond
Smith, Jeff

Spartanburg County
Bivins, Patrick
Brown, Green

Davis, Isom
Green, Richard
Gregory, Coleman
Hobson, Sylvester
Jenkins, Jeff
Wilson, Hammett

Sumter County
Cooper, Daniel
Wilson, Robert

Union County
Dawkins, John
Gregory, John
Lindsay, E. J.
Murphy, Jim
Porter, James
Robinson, Green
Sartor, Alex

Williamsburg County
Brogdon, William
Chandler, Caesar
McBride, Porter
McCrea, Peter
McCullough, Anthony
McCutcheson, George
Pressley, John
Shaw, Joe
Washington, Ned

York County
Crawford, Peter, *Catawba*
Marshall, Heywood, *York, Rt. 3*
Melton, George, *York*
McKey, Jeff, *Catawba Junction*
Sanders, Sam, *Filbert*

Appendix C—Frank Rangs

Not all South Carolina African Americans who were attached to Confederate service applied for or received pensions from the state. Joseph Gainey of Spartanburg shared the following account with the author.

According to the *Greenville News* of 29 August 1930 (section 2, page 21,columns 2-4), Frank Rangs, aged 93 years, not only had accompanied his young master Hut Boler from Newberry into Civil War service but also had served with Gen. Robert E. Lee. According to Rangs, he entered service with Boler and served until Boler lost his right arm. Boler and Rangs then returned to Newberry, and Jim Boler, the younger Boler's father, again sent Rangs to serve with the Army of Northern Virginia. At that time, Rangs began cooking and washing for General Lee. Rangs' service ended at Appomattox.

Preliminary checking located a James M. Boland (1841–1922) of Newberry County who served in Confederate forces. Boland has a CSA marker and is buried in Hinson Cemetery near Pomaria.[1]

1. Newberry County, South Carolina Cemeteries, comp. and ed George Carter Abrams, v. 1 (Newberry: Newberry County Historical Society, 1982), 136.

Appendix D—South Carolina's Confederate Pensioners on the 1920 Soundex

Compiled by Ruth S. Green and Dolly Wells

Information on the United States Census is closed to the public for 72 years after it is created. Consequently, the 1920 Census is the latest one available. The Federal Government uses a SOUNDEX approach to index this schedule for South Carolina. The Soundex is specially coded so that variant spellings are usually indexed together.

The following list details the Soundex entries for South Carolina Confederate pensioners. This list is incomplete. Some individuals were not enumerated and others, perhaps, were enumerated but not indexed. The entries include the name of the pensioner; the Soundex code for that surname; the pensioner's age, birthplace, and residence; other family members living in the household; a reference to the South Carolina 1920 population schedule, and, in a few instances, a reference to the 1900 or 1910 Soundex to help the genealogical researcher locate the actual entry on the census. Only those individuals whose county of residence matches the pension applicant's residence and whose age is reasonable for the service described in the abstract are listed. The information below has been taken from microfilm, which can be difficult to read. Researchers, therefore, are advised to verify the information.

ABELL, Anderson (A140): aged 75; residence—Blythewood Road, Richland County; enumerated with Mag Abell aged 70 and Lucy Graham aged 38. (E. D. 117, sheet 4, line 26)

ABERCROMBIE, Thomas (A162): aged 79; residence—Laurens County. (E. D. 50, sheet 6, line 48)

ABRAHAM, Neaton (A165): aged 78; residence—Lee County; enumerated with Christiana Abraham aged 67. (E. D. 21, sheet 6, line 99)

ALBERT, Henry (A416): aged 75; residence—42 Hayward Street, Bishopville, SC; enumerated with Nelson Williams. (E. D. 14, sheet 4, line 24)

ALFORD (?Alfred), Thomas M. (A416): aged 80; residence—McCormick County; enumerated with Isabelle Alford aged 70 and Janie Talbert aged 16. (E. D. 103, sheet 9, line 9)

ALSTON, James (A423): aged 77; residence—Berkeley; enumerated with Jane Alston aged 69. Christopher Alston aged 34, Richard Norton aged 12, and Arnal Robinson aged 9. (E. D. 39, sheet 7, line 96)

ANDERSON, George (A536): aged 69; residence—Laurens County;

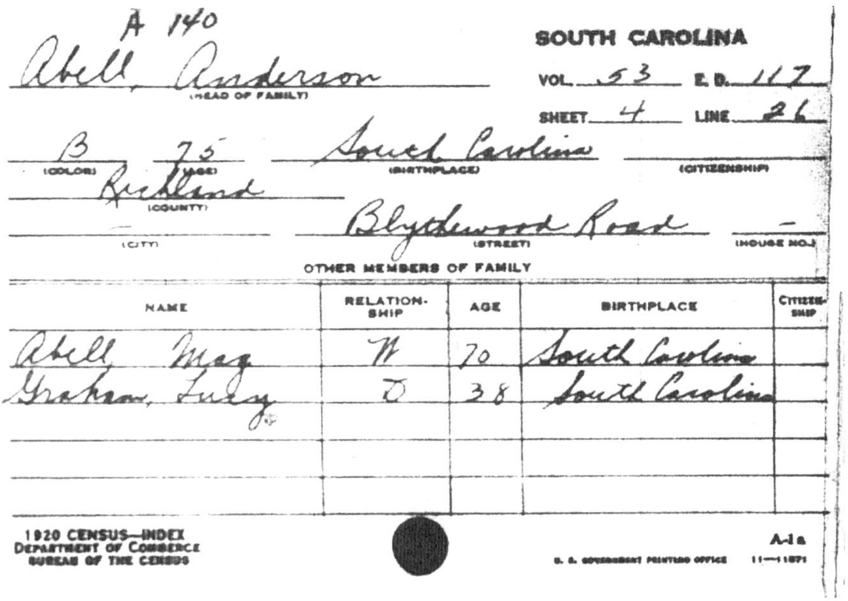
A 140

SOUTH CAROLINA

Abell, Anderson (HEAD OF FAMILY) VOL. 53 E. D. 117 SHEET 4 LINE 26

B (COLOR) 75 (AGE) South Carolina (BIRTHPLACE) (CITIZENSHIP)

Richland (COUNTY)

— (CITY) Blythewood Road (STREET) — (HOUSE NO.)

OTHER MEMBERS OF FAMILY

NAME	RELATIONSHIP	AGE	BIRTHPLACE	CITIZENSHIP
Abell, May	W	70	South Carolina	
Graham, Lucy	D	38	South Carolina	

1920 CENSUS—INDEX
DEPARTMENT OF COMMERCE
BUREAU OF THE CENSUS

A-1a
U. S. GOVERNMENT PRINTING OFFICE 11—11871

Soundex entry for Anderson Abell.

enumerated with Benjamin Anderson. (E. D. 71, sheet 9, line 90)

BALDERICK, Abraham (B436): aged 70; residence—Orangeburg County; enumerated with Miley Thompson aged 60, Isiah Thompson aged 15, Mattie Thompson aged 10, and Murie Williams aged 18. (E. D. 57, sheet 17, line 45)

BARRETT, Emmett (B630): aged 75; residence 709 Sumter Street, Aiken, SC. (E. D. 131, sheet 4, line 50)

BING, Thomas (B520): aged 99; residence—Hampton County; enumerated with Rachel Bing aged 80. (E. D. 103, sheet 10, line 40)

BLACK, Jeff (B420): aged 70 (the age does not agree with the death certificate); residence—Abbeville County; enumerated with John Black (E. D. 15, sheet 7, line 2)

BOWLES, Sam (B420): aged 74; residence—Beaufort County, enumerated with George Bowles aged 35. (E. D. 65, sheet 4, line 62)

BOYD, Richard S. (B300): aged 75; residence—Peak Road, Lexington County; enumerated with Missouri Boyd aged 64 and Willis L. Kirklin aged 19. (E. D. 28, sheet 3, line 45)

BRISTOW, Comodore (B623): aged 65 (this age does not agree with the death certificate); residence—Barnwell County; enumerated with Mary J. Singleton. (E. D. 49, sheet 18, line 78)

BROWN, Zacarias (B650): aged 81; residence—Fairfield County; enumerated with Lucy Brown aged 65, Robert Brown aged 19, and Queen Elizabeth Brown aged 15. (E. D. 52, sheet 11, line 82)

BURNSIDES, Sam (B652): aged 75; residence Lisbon Church Road, Laurens County; enumerated with Eliza Burnsides aged 65, Lillie May Rodgers aged 16, and Mary Rodgers aged 6 months. (E. D. 61, sheet 7, line 38)

BUTLER, Edd (B346): aged 75; residence—Greenwood County; enumerated with Queen Butler aged 60 and Edd Butler aged 43. (E. D. 83, sheet 6, line 75)

BOYKIN, William (B250): aged 83; residence—Kershaw County; enumerated with Betsy Boykin aged 60. (E. D. 73, sheet 7, line 51)

BIVINGS, Patrick (B152): aged 74; residence—Spartanburg County; enumerated with Jamie Bivings aged 64 and George Bivings aged 18 (E. D. 76, sheet 16, line 26)

CAMPBELL, Paul (C514): aged 75; residence—Charleston County; (E. D. 29, sheet 13, line 3)

CANNON, Josh (C550): aged 80; residence—Newberry County; enumerated with John Sweetenberg (E. D. 127, sheet 2, line 36)

CANNON, Preston (C550): aged 70; residence—Newberry County; enumerated with Fannie May Cannon aged 14. (E. D. 116, sheet 1, line 31)

CARMICHAEL, Elijah (C652): aged 75; residence—Dillon County; enumerated with Clarkie Carmichael aged 50, Ornetta Carmichael aged 23, Jake Carmichael aged 20, Etha Carmichael aged 18, and Esther Carmichael aged 4. (E. D. 68, sheet 4, line 63)

CHAVIS, Ransom (C120): aged 75; residence—Richland County; enumerated with Sarah Chavis aged 71. (E. D. 172, sheet 13, line 6)

COHEN, Abe, Sr. (C500): aged 75; residence—Newberry County; enumerated with Abe Cohen, Jr. (E. D. 120, sheet 12, line 34)

COLEMAN, William P. (C455): aged 72; residence—Fairfield County; enumerated with Ellen Coleman aged 61 and Pinkey Coleman aged 5. (E. D. 50, sheet 5, line 3)

COPELAND, Spencer (C145): aged 82; residence—20 Ardmore, Clinton, SC; enumerated with Emma Copeland aged 63 and Irby Copeland aged 29. (E. D. 56, sheet 17, line 99)

CROSS, Council (C620): aged 65 (age does not agree with his death certificate); residence—Williston, Barnwell County; enumerated with Emily

George Briggs, Confederate pensioner from Union County, died in March 1944. No pension application exists for Briggs at the state level, and he does not appear on the 1926 list. Joseph Gainey.

McCreavy aged 111; Emelia Moody aged 7, Henry Balls aged 25 and Lottie Balls aged 25. (E. D. 61, sheet 7, line 57)

DANIELS, Marcus (D542): aged 73; residence—Barnwell County; enumerated with Cloe Daniel aged 60 and Jerome Daniels aged 24. (E. D. 55, sheet 3, line 12)

DARBY, Newton (D610): aged 75; residence—Newberry County. (E. D. 127, sheet 8, line 69)

DATTS, Lazarus (D320): aged 78; residence—Third Street, Estill, SC; enumerated with Henry L. Solomons (E. D. 101, sheet 4, line 61)

DAVIS, Henry (D120): aged 75; residence—Fairfield County; enumerated with Ella Davis aged 65 and Ben Davis aged 23. (E. D. 68, sheet 5, line 46)

DAVIS, June (D120): aged 86; residence—Hampton County; enumerated with Mathew Davis. (E. D. 108, sheet 13, line 82)

DEAN, Elias (D500): aged 85; residence—Greenwood County; enumerated with Amanda Dean aged 65. (E. D. 83, sheet 2, line 49)

DEAN, Henry (D500): aged 69; residence—Spartanburg County. (E. D. 77, sheet 17, line 44)

DELOACH, Richard (D420): aged 79; residence—Allendale and Barnwell Road, Allendale County. (E. D. 28, sheet 3, line 78)

DONLEY, Ben (D540): aged 74; residence—Marion, SC; enumerated with Mary C. Donley aged 42. (E. D. 102, sheet 23, line 44)

DRAYTON, Isaac (D635): aged 85; residence—48 Vanderhorst Street, Charleston, SC; enumerated with Sarah Drayton aged 70. (E. D. 44, sheet 10, line 44)

DRUMMONDS, Milton (D635): aged 73; residence—183 Stevens Street, Spartanburg, SC; enumerated with Mary Drummond aged 56, Fletcher Drummond aged 25, George Drummond aged 23, Sula Drummond aged 17, and Roswell Drummond aged 13. (E. D. 118, sheet 22, line 69)

ELLIOTT, Gasse (E430): aged 74; born Virginia; residence—Aiken County; enumerated with Lizie Elliott aged 68. (E. D. 20, sheet 4, line 31)

FLOYD, Henty (F430): aged 78; residence—Barnwell County; enumerated with Minnie Floyd aged 65 and Vise Floyd aged 14. (E. D. 54, sheet 13, line 94)

FOOTMAN, Josh (F355): aged 85; residence—Dorchester County; enumerated with Hana Footman aged 46. (E. D. 66, sheet 10, line 62)

FORD, Edwin (F630): aged 63; residence—Hilbert Road, Georgetown County; enumerated with Clara Ford aged 65, Edward G. Ford aged 44, Julia D. Ford aged 24, and Lottie Stack aged 14. (E. D. 65, sheet 6, line 22)

FORD, Henry J. (F630): aged 84; residence—Plantersville Road, Georgetown County; enumerated with Flora Ford aged 81 and Mary Ford aged 7. (E. D. 74, sheet 8, line 41)

FOXWORTH, William H. (F263): aged 73; residence—Marion County; enumerated with Annie A. Foxworth aged 60, David C. Foxworth aged 18 and Retta M. Foxworth aged 17. (E. D. 114, sheet 12, line 63)

FRANKLIN, Twist (F652): aged 77; residence—Marion County; enumerated with Hannah Franklin aged 67, Eliza Franklin aged 36, Liston Franklin aged 28, Lardo Franklin aged 21, Chester Donly aged 5, and Lawrence Donly aged 2 months. (E. D. 113, sheet 1, line 42)

FRANKS, Bennie (F652): aged 90; residence—Laurens County. (E. D. 50, sheet 4, line 22)

FRAZIER, Mark (F626): aged 70; residence—19 Harrisburg Street, Abbeville, SC. (E. D. 3, sheet 2, line 28)

FUNCHES, July (F522): aged 70; residence—Holliman Bridge Road, Orangeburg County; enumerated with Louzina Funches aged 42, Jacob Funches aged 24, Dollie Funches aged 19, Samuel Funches aged 16, Fred Funches aged 14, Louzina Funches aged 11, and Walter Funches aged 3 months. (E. D. 78, sheet 7, line 6)

GANTT, Edward (G530): aged 75; residence—Barnwell County; enumerated with Ellen Gantt aged 75, Emeline Gantt aged 30, Ellen Gantt, Jr., aged 20, Willie May Gantt aged 18, Boot Henderson aged 13, and Clara May Powell aged 8. (E. D. 57, sheet 6, line 65)

GANTT, Jake (G530): aged 70; residence—Aiken County; enumerated with Marie Gantt aged 60, Venis Gantt aged 27, and Dortey Gantt aged 23. (E. D. 17, sheet 2, line 8)

GILLIARD, Philip (G463): aged 77; residence—Plantersville Road, Georgetown; enumerated with Liza Gilliard aged 17, Minie Gilliard aged 15, and June Gillard aged 13. (E. D. 59, sheet 9, line 56)

GLOVER, Frank (G416): aged 73; residence—Two Chop Road, Orangeburg County; enumerated with Nellie Glover aged 48. (E. D. 72, sheet 20, line 3)

GRANT, Alfred (G653): aged 78; residence—West side, Puckett Road, Laurens County; enumerated with Isaac McGowin aged 75. (E. D. 148, sheet 1, line 61)

GRANT, Fred (G653): aged 75; residence—Abbeville County; enumerated with Sarah Grant aged 68. (E. D. 2, sheet 1, line 42)

GRANT, Wesley (G653): aged 79; residence—Laurens County. (E. D. 49, sheet 22, line 97)

GREENE, Jacob (G650): aged 78; residence—Railroad Avenue, Cheraw, SC; enumerated with Ellen Greene aged 68 and Lula Greene aged 16. (E. D. 36, sheet 26, line 75)

GRICE, Joe (G620): aged 76; residence—12 Fourth Avenue, Dillon, SC. (E. D. 33, sheet 4, line 12)

GRIFFIN, Benjamin P. (G615): aged 72; residence—Pickens County; enumerated with Sarah T. Griffin aged 65, Elisha H. Griffin aged 39, and Charles C. Griffin aged 6. (E. D. 165, sheet 10, line 61)

GUNTER, Harry (G536): aged 70; residence—604 Gates Street, Columbia, SC; enumerated with Jane Gunter aged 60 and Alice Gunter aged 20. (E. D. 79, sheet 32, line 98)

GYLES, James (G420): aged 80; residence—133 Wentworth Street, Charleston, SC; enumerated with Mary E. Gyles aged 70. (E. D. 29, sheet 11, line 80)

HAINES, Jenkin (H520): aged 80; residence—Hampton County; enumerated with Robert Haines. (E. D. 104, sheet 37, line 78)

HAY, Cato (H000): aged 87; residence—Barnwell County; enumerated with Ann Hay aged 75 and Sam Cave aged 17. (vol. 8, sheet 16, line 37)

HALTYWANGER, Abe (H435): aged 73; residence—Newberry County; enumerated with Mary Haltiwanger aged 50. (E. D. 112, sheet 2, line 56)

HAMPTON, Jim (H513): aged 84; residence—Anderson County; enumerated with Joe Hampton aged 62, Gertrude Hampton aged 19, and Nancy Hampton aged 8 months. (E. D. 30, sheet 8, line 15)

HARDY, Derry (H630: aged 75; residence—Sampit Road, Georgetown County; enumerated with Gussie Hardy aged 30, Willie Hardy aged 21, Gertrude Hardy aged 6, and Luesmay Hardy aged 5. (E. D. 68, sheet 21, line 11)

HARMON, John (H655): aged 75; residence—Irmo Road, Richland County; enumerated with Lila Harmon aged 75 and Will Gregor aged 9. (E. D. 122, sheet 1, line 88)

HARRELL, Sipipo (H640): aged 70; residence—Bay Street, Mullins, SC; enumerated with Roseatta McLellan. (E. D. 112, sheet 2, line 14)

HARRIS, Henry (H620): aged 83; residence—Oconee County; enumerated with Bettis Harris aged 68, Gertrude Sitton aged 26, Donat Sitton aged 7 and Ally Sitton aged 2. (E. D. 143, sheet 5, line 43)

HARRIS, Joseph, Sr. (H620): aged 86; residence—Saluda Road, Saluda County; enumerated with Lucy Harris aged 85. (E. D. 128, sheet 12, line 34)

HARRISON, Warren (H625): aged 62; residence—Ninety Six, SC; enumerated with Semira Harrison aged 57 and Hattie Simmons aged 9. (E. D. 85, sheet 7, line 68)

HART, Tilman (H630): aged 77; residence—6 Lee Avenue, Johnston, SC; enumerated with Fannie Hart aged 45, Alberta Hart aged 24, Richard Hart aged 27, and Otis Hart aged 8. (E. D. 88, sheet 12, line 15)

HAY, Cato (H000): aged 87; residence—Barnwell County; enumerated with Ann Hay aged 75 and Sam Cave aged 17. (E. D. 49, sheet 16, line 37)

HENRY, Addison (H560): aged 67; residence—Laurens County; enumerated with Bertha Henry aged 55, Mamie Henry aged 23, Leroy Henry aged 5, John C. Henry aged 2, and Estelle Henry aged 8. (E. D. 71, sheet 9, line 34)

HINTON, Joe (H535): aged 86; residence—Camden Road, Richland County; enumerated with Primus Edison. (E. D. 104, sheet 18, line 75)

HOBSON, Sylvester (H125): aged 70; residence—178 East Hampton Avenue, Spartanburg, SC; enumerated with Cornelia Hobson aged 65, Emma Smith aged 30, Garland Smith aged 10, Herman Smith aged 9, and Oscar Smith aged 7. (E. D. 110, sheet 14, line 74)

HODGES, George (H322): aged 70; residence—Greenville County; enumerated with Nancy Hodges aged 63. (E. D. 2, sheet 3, line 32)

HOLMES, Gilbert (H452): aged 68; residence—Bull Swamp Road, Orangeburg County; enumerated with Clarra Holmes aged 65 and Bessie Holmes aged 20. (E. D. 66, sheet 1, line 25)

HOOD, Thomas (H300): aged 73; residence—815 Sullivan Street, Laurens, SC; enumerated with Heywood Hood. (E. D. 64, sheet 10, line 57)

HOOK, William (H200); aged 65; residence—126 1/2 East Russell Street, Orangeburg, SC. (E. D. 49, sheet 2, line 30)

HOWARD, Steven (H630): aged 82; residence—Old Charleston Road, Saluda County; enumerated with Luke Howard. (E. D. 127, sheet 4, line 19)

HOWELL, Emanuel (H400): aged 86; residence—341 Pauling Quarter, St. Matthews, SC; enumerated with Jennie Howell aged 70. (E. D. 3, sheet 5, line 32)

JAGERS, Charles (J262): aged 88; residence—1313 Oak Street, Columbia, SC; enumerated with Hariott Jagers aged 63 and Elloise Jagers aged 15. (E. D. 94, sheet 14, line 89)

JENKINS, Esau (J525): aged 83; residence—Dorchester County; enumerated with Mary Jenkins aged 55. (E. D. 146, sheet 10, line 190

JONES, Henry (J520): aged 75; residence—Abbeville County; enumerated with Lizzy Jones aged 50, Lula Jones aged 14, Willie Jones aged 14, Clemmie Jones aged 13, and Sammie Jones aged 10. (E. D. 17, sheet 10, line 60)

JONES, William (J520): aged 68 (age does not agree with death certificate); residence—Orangeburg County; enumerated with Martha Jones aged 22 and Ben Lawton aged 6. (E. D. 43, sheet 6, line 30)

JOHNSON, Edward (J525): aged 65; residence—Calhoun County; enumerated with Rebecca Johnson aged 55 and Marion Felder aged 16. (E. D. 8, sheet 11, line 40)

JOHNSON, Hector (J535): aged 84; residence—Dorchester County; enumerated with Celia Johnson aged 15, P. Johnson aged 10, Shephard Johnson aged 9, Paul Johnson aged 6 and Silas Johnson aged 6. (E. D. 144, sheet 11, line 66)

JOHNSON, Noah (J525): aged 87; residence—1020 Bryant Street, Columbia, SC; enumerated with Lizzie Johnson aged 45 and Martha Johnson aged 16. (E. D. 95, sheet 28, line 7)

KEARSE, Preston (K620): aged 77; residence—Bamberg County; enumerated with Paulie Kearse aged 55, Shalee Kearse aged 24, Span Kearse aged 18, and Fannie Daniels aged 90. (E. D. 42, sheet 1, line 65)

KELLEY, Ansel (K400): aged 74; residence—Aiken County; enumerated with Pusan Kelley aged 70 and Canary Kelley aged 13. (E. D. 22, sheet 18, line 95)

LARK, Summers (L620): aged 96; residence—Chappells Town, SC; enumerated with Solomon Basher. (E. D. 120, sheet 15, line 17)

LAUREL, William (L640): aged 75; residence—Jasper County; enumerated with Louise Laurel aged 40, Gussie Laurel aged 16, Hilton Laurel aged 11, Lillie M. Laurel aged 16, Moselle Laurel aged 10, and Allisa Laurel aged 7. (E. D. 110, sheet 7, line 88)

LEMON, Willis (L550): aged 72; residence—Dorchester County; enumerated with D. Lemon aged 30, Lucy Lemon aged 28, and others. (E. D. 124, sheet 15, line 23)

LOGAN, Wess (L250): aged 70; residence—Greenwood County; enumerated with Aggie Logan aged 45 and James Logan aged 1. (E. D. 83, sheet 4, line 42)

LOUDHOLT, Miles L. (L343): aged 77; residence—Allendale County. (E. D. 33, sheet 1, line 60)

LOYD, Chance (L200): aged 70; residence—Barnwell County; enumerated with Algeram Loyd aged 70, Chany Loyd aged 17, and Walter Rice aged 8. (E. D. 12, sheet 16, line 66)

MACK, Samuel (M200): aged 65; residence—279 Ashley Avenue, Charleston, SC; enumerated with Emms Mack aged 50 and Odessa Mack aged 16. (E. D. 71, sheet 11, line 4)

MATTISON, Marshall (M325): aged 65; residence—Anderson County; enumerated with Fannie Mattison aged 55. (E. D. 24, sheet 10, line 3)

MCCLINTIC, Perry (M245): aged 78; residence—22 North Bell Street, Clinton, SC; enumerated with Isibell McClintic aged 80 and Willie M. McClintic aged 22. (E. D. 57, sheet 11, line 19)

MCCLINTON, Jack (M245): aged 74; residence—Abbeville County; enumerated with Ellen McClinton aged 52 and Patsy Smith aged 12. (E. D. 13, sheet 18, line 27)

MCDONALD, Bistow (M235): aged 65 (age does not agree with death certificate); residence—Lynches River Road, Bishopville, SC; enumerated with Sue McDonald aged 58, Carrie B. McDonald aged 25, Caroline McDonald aged 18, and James Samson aged 10. (E. D. 17, sheet 25, line 52)

MCELRETH, Tom M. (M246): aged 79; residence—Buncombe Road, Spartanburg County; enumerated with Carrie McElreth aged 53, Tom McElreth, Jr. aged 24, L. P. McElreth aged 15, Lewence McElreth aged 13, and Tuts McElreth aged 20. (E. D. 125, sheet 18, line 94)

MCNEIL, Hector (M254): aged 70; residence—New Hudson Street, Dillon, SC; enumerated with Rosebell McNeil aged 72. (E. D. 33, sheet 20, line 30)

MIKELL, Walace (M240): aged 70; residence—195 Ashley Avenue, Charleston, SC; enumerated with Joseph Mikell aged 14 and Edward Mikell aged 10. (E. D. 46. 12, sheet 12, line 40)

MILAN, Nelson (M450): aged 74; residence—Laurens County; enumerated with Martha Milan aged 66. (E. D. 48, sheet 6, line 82)

MILEY, James (M400): aged 70; residence—931 Fairfield Street, Aiken, SC; enumerated with Sallie Miley aged 50. (E. D. 4, sheet 11, line 31)

MILLER, Kelly (M460): aged 95; residence—Fairfield County; enumerated with Henry Miller. (E. D. 63, sheet 7, line 75)

MIMS, Dallas (M520): aged 80; residence—McCormick County; enumerated with Bettie Mims aged 55. (E. D. 34, sheet 6, line 24)

MITCHELL, June (M324): aged 75; residence—Dickson Street, Orangeburg, SC; enumerated with Claire Mitchell aged 19, Sammie Mitchell aged 19, Lonnie Mitchell aged 18, and Henry Mitchell aged 15. (E. D. unreadable, sheet 11, line unreadable)

MOORE, Hirem (M600): aged 72; residence—Fairfield County; enumerated with Eliza Moore aged 63, Lila Moore aged 15, Rufs Moore aged 19 and Fannie Moore aged 7. (E. D. 64, sheet 4, line 5)

MORGAN, Alfred (M625): aged 72; residence—Newberry County; enumerated with Hassie Morgan aged 40. (E. D. 105, sheet 4, line 65)

MURPHY, Robert (M610): aged 84; residence—Kershaw County; enumerated with Ellen Murphy aged 50 and Era Murphy aged 16. (E. D. 80, sheet 30, line 99)

OWENS, Starling (O520): aged 80; residence—Anderson County; enumerated with Sarah Owens aged 76 and Fred Owens aged 28. (E. D. 42, sheet 12, line 44)

PAGE, Alred (P200): aged 70; residence—Marion County; enumerated with Alice Page aged 66 and John Page aged 12. (E. D. 100, sheet 4, line 48)

PITTS, Hezzie, Sr. (P320): aged 75; residence—Newberry County; enumerated with Hezzie Pitts, Jr. (E. D. 120, sheet 9, line 39)

POLITE, Paul (P430): aged 86; residence—Jasper County; enumerated with Mollie Polite aged 75 and Corren Chamie aged 15. (E. D. 112, sheet 11, line 57)

POU, Lewis (P000): aged 69; residence—Third Street, North, SC; enumerated with Mary A. Pou aged 65, Peter Pou aged 13, Leroy Brooks aged 12, and Nuna Brooks aged 7. (E. D. 54, sheet 3, line 59)

PRINCE, Hiram (P652): aged 70; residence—Orangeburg County; enumerated with Hattie Prince aged 37, Mary Prince aged 16, Morris Prince aged 13, and Jasper Prince aged 11. (E. D. 52, sheet 7, line 76)

PRINGLE, Aron (P652): aged 87; residence—Choppee Road, Georgetown County; enumerated with Elizabeth Pringle aged 60, Arthur Pringle aged 48, Viola Pringle aged 16, and Lettie Pringle aged 13. (E. D. 74, sheet 18, line 31)

QUARLES, Hawk (Q642): aged 70; residence—Aiken County; enumerated with Nacy Quarles aged, Fannie Quarles aged 27, Casie Quarles aged 10, Minnie Quarles aged 6, and John H. Quarles age 1. (E. D. 8, sheet 15, line 9)

QUARLES, Richard (Q642): aged 73; residence—McCormick County; enumerated with Haseltine Quarles aged 60. (E. D. 95, sheet 16, line 77)

REAVES, Sim (R120): aged 78; residence—Dillon County. (E. D. 23, sheet 9, line 21)

REED, Yancy (R300): aged 65 (age does not agree with death certificate); residence—121 Cambridge Street, Abbeville, SC; enumerated with Jane Reed aged 60. (E. D. 3, sheet 10, line 18)

RHODES, Primas (R320): aged 86; residence—Laurens County; enumerated with Harry Rhodes aged 60, Etolia Rhodes aged 22, Bob Rhodes aged 21, Homer Rhodes aged 17, Laura Rhodes aged 18, and Liddie Rhodes aged 2. (E. D. 51, sheet 17, line 34)

RILLEY, William (R400): aged 74; residence—Bowman, SC; enumerated with Julia Rilley aged 48, Ed Rilley aged 23, Noble Rilley aged 22, Mary Jane Rilley aged 18, Sarah Riley aged 16, Mary Rilley aged 13, and Martha Rilley aged 13. (E. D. 43, sheet 17, line 96)

ROACH, Aaron (R200): aged 70; residence—Abbeville County; enumerated with Mandy Roach aged 68 and Fred Roach aged 16, (E. D. 7, sheet 8, line 78)

RUFF, Sanker (R100): aged 65; residence—Kirkland Avenue, Eau Claire, SC. (E. D. 96, sheet 15, line 64)

SCOTT, Caesar (S300); aged 84; residence—Beaufort County; enumerated with Frank Scott. (E. D. 75, sheet 10, line 32)

SINGLETON, Benjamin (S524): aged 72; residence—419 Scott Street, Beaufort, SC; enumerated with Julia Singleton aged 68. (E. D. 66, sheet 9, line 72)

SMITH, Frank (S530): aged 70; residence—Bamberg County; enumerated with Catherine Smith aged 64, Longs Smith aged 31, and Bertha Smith aged 18. (E. D. 44, sheet 10, line 17)

SPEED, Luther (S130): aged 75; residence—Scott Road, Abbeville County; enumerated with Charlie Johnson. (E. D. 16, sheet 7, line 4)

SPENCER, George (S152): aged 75; residence—Abbeville County; enumerated with Rachel Spencer aged 60 and John Spencer aged 13. (E. D. 2, sheet 2, line 80)

SULLIVAN, Milton (S415): aged 70; residence—Greenwood County; enumerated with Elizabeth Sullivan aged 60 and Alberta Sullivan aged 14. (E. D. 74, sheet 6, line 68)

SWINTON, Paul (S535): aged 90; residence—Orangeburg County. (E. D. 59, sheet 13, line 42)

THOMAS, Ben (T520): aged 67; residence—56 Buena Vista Avenue, North Augusta, SC; enumerated with Caroline Thomas aged 70. (E. D. 19, sheet 6, line 1)

THOMAS, Charles (T520): aged 65; residence—Church Street East, Branchville, SC; enumerated with Maria Thomas aged 65 and Lillie Smith aged 21. (E. D. 45, sheet 17, line 1)

TILLEY, James (T400): aged 79; residence—Calhoun County; enumerated with Julia Tilley aged 65, Maggie Tilley aged 30, Julius Tilley aged 25, Herbert Tillery aged 20, and Shelly Tilley aged 3. (E. D. 8, sheet 7, line 16)

TILLMAN, Reubin (T455): aged 65; residence—Edgefield County; enumerated with Laura Bright aged 60. (E. D. 90, sheet 17, line 55)

TOMPKINS, Mat (T512): aged 75; residence—McCormick County, enumerated with Rachel Tompkins aged 70 and Joe Tompkins aged 12. (E. D. 102, sheet 11, line 58)

TOWNSEND, Dock (T525): aged 74; residence—Marlboro County; enumerated with Robert Steward. (E. D. 121, sheet 5, line 54)

VARINE, Wesley (V650): aged 86; residence—Choppee Road, Georgetown County; enumerated with Ellen Varine aged 61. (E. D. 74, sheet 13, line 55)

WALKER, Jerry (W426): aged 80; residence—Barnwell County; enumerated with Henry Etta Walker aged 80. (E. D. 53, sheet 16, line 99)

WALKER, Peter (W426): aged 70 (age does not agree with death certificate): residence—23 Bull Street, Orangeburg, SC; enumerated with Carrie Walker aged 65, (E. D. 47, sheet 7, line 31)

WALLACE, Marshall (W420): aged 68; residence—Caldwell Street, Newberry, SC; enumerated with John Wallace aged 50. (E. D. 110, sheet 14, line 96)

WASHINGTON, Jacob (W252): aged 76; residence—Hampton County; enumerated with Loula Washington aged 45, Madaline Washington aged 13, Cornelius Washington aged 19, Jacob Washington aged 18, Lonnie Washington aged 7, and others. (E. D. 108, sheet 15, line 59)

WASHINGTON, Nias (W252): aged 99; residence—Newberry County; enumerated with Sarah Washington aged 68; Cornelius Washington aged 18. (E. D. 119, sheet 11, line 12)

WASHINGTON, Sam (W252): aged 75; residence—537 Washington Street, Laurens, SC; enumerated with Mary Washington aged 70 and Luther Washington aged 17. (E. D. 64, sheet 4, line 81)

WASHINGTON, William (W252): aged 76; residence—Greenwood County; enumerated with Henretta Washington aged 60; Agnes Washington aged 22; John Washington aged 20, Sadie Burnes aged 21, and Walter Solomon aged 22. (E. D. 75, sheet 11, line 52)

WILLIAMS, Alexander (W452): aged 56 in 1900; residence —Abbeville County; enumerated with Martha Williams aged 42. (1900 E. D. 12, sheet 9, line 76)

WILLIAMS, Alexander (W452): aged 50 in 1900; residence—Fairfield Street, Aiken, SC; enumerated with Catherine Williams aged 45, Solomon Williams aged 17, Abraham Williams aged 16, Samie aged 8, David aged 6, and others. (1900 E. D. 22, sheet 20, line 8)

WILLIAMS, Ambrose (W452): aged 54 in 1900; residence—Newberry County; enumerated with Susan Williams aged 46. (1900 E. D. 89, sheet 4, line 46)

WILLIAMS, Bram (W452): aged 61 in 1900; residence—Barnwell County; enumerated with Jane Williams aged 44, Bertha Williams aged 11, and Janie Williams aged 5. (1900 E. D. 21, sheet 10, line 80)

Alex Sartor, Union County pensioner. Although no pension application exists for Sartor on the state level, he appears on the 1926 pension list. A few years ago, the General States Rights Gist Camp, Sons of Confederate Veterans, marked Sartor's grave. Joseph Gainey.

WILLIAMS, Green W. (W452): aged 62 in 1900; residence—Richland County; enuemrated with Sarah Williams aged 50 and Nelson Harris aged 46. (1900 E. D. 80, sheet 1, line 12)

WILLIAMS, Henry (W452): aged 78; residence—Cooley Bridge Road, Greenville County; enumerated with Matilda Williams aged 67, Tinfrie A. Williams aged 30, Gladys Williams aged 14, Hattie M. Williams aged 10, and James Williams aged 7 months. (E. D. 40, sheet 11, line 18)

WINGATE, Washington (W523): aged 64 in 1900; residence—Chesterfield County; enumerated with Rising Wingate aged 55; Catharine Wingate aged 25, Amanda Wingate aged 22, Thomas Wingate aged 10, Maggie Wingate aged 15, and others. (1900 E. D. 17, sheet 12, line 32)

WISE, Lewis (W200): aged 63 in 1910; residence—Barnwell County; enumerated with Lorene Wise aged 38, Love Wise aged 1, Guss Wise aged 28, Clarence Wise aged 19, Elzie Wise aged 16, Henderson Wise aged 15, and Lottie Wise aged 7. (1910 E. D. 40, sheet 9)

WRIGHT, Johnson (W623); aged 63 in 1900; residence—Oconee County; enumerated with Mary Wright aged 9, Gus Wright aged 7, David Brown aged 35, Lucy Brown aged 35, Lucinda Brown aged 11, and others. (1900 E.D. 73, sheet 11, line 21)

YOUMANS, John (Y552): aged 60; residence—Hampton County; enumerated with Patiens Youmans aged 50 and Douglas Youmans aged 21. (E. D. 106, sheet 19, line 33)

YOUNG, Limus C. (Y520): aged 70; residence—Old State Road, Orangeburg County; enumerated with Pressy Young aged 27. (E. D. 64, sheet 8, line 63)

YOUNG, Ross (Y520): aged 77; residence—Sandy Ford Road, Laurens County; enumerated with Lucinda Young aged 71. (E. D. 62, sheet 6, line 82)

Index

C

D

E

F

G

H

I

J

K

N

O

P

Q

R

S

T

U

V

W

Y

Z